How to Reach Enlightenment

Polly Campbell

Teach ®
Yourself

How to Reach Enlightenment

Polly Campbell

Hodder Education

338 Euston Road, London NW1 3BH.

Hodder Education is an Hachette UK company

First published in UK 2012 by Hodder Education

First published in US 2012 by The McGraw-Hill Companies, Inc.

This edition published 2012

Copyright © 2012 Polly Campbell

The moral rights of the author have been asserted

Database right Hodder Education (makers)

The Teach Yourself name is a registered trademark of Hachette UK.

British Library Cataloguing in Publication Data: a catalogue record for this title is available from the British Library.

Library of Congress Catalog Card Number: on file.

10 9 8 7 6 5 4 3 2 1

The publisher has used its best endeavours to ensure that any website addresses referred to in this book are correct and active at the time of going to press. However, the publisher and the author have no responsibility for the websites and can make no guarantee that a site will remain live or that the content will remain relevant, decent or appropriate.

The publisher has made every effort to mark as such all words which it believes to be trademarks. The publisher should also like to make it clear that the presence of a word in the book, whether marked or unmarked, in no way affects its legal status as a trademark.

Every reasonable effort has been made by the publisher to trace the copyright holders of material in this book. Any errors or omissions should be notified in writing to the publisher, who will endeavour to rectify the situation for any reprints and future editions.

Hachette UK's policy is to use papers that are natural, renewable and recyclable products and made from wood grown in sustainable forests. The logging and manufacturing processes are expected to conform to the environmental regulations of the country of origin.

www.hoddereducation.co.uk

Cover image © Irina Tischenko - Fotolia

Typeset by Cenveo Publisher Services.

Printed in Great Britain by CPI Group (UK) Ltd, Croydon, CR0 4YY.

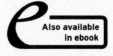

Contents

Meet the author

When I was eight years old, all I wanted was to win the bicycle in the window of the newspaper office. If I could sell the most newspaper subscriptions, it would be mine. That goal became a reality, but even then winning the bicycle seemed more than an external mark of achievement: it showed there was a powerful energy at work.

As a child, I didn't know what this energy was, but I did know that I wanted to be a part of it. I wanted to connect to the energy that created the stars and the frogs croaking on a rainy spring day. What I know now, as an adult, is that I am *always* connected to all of that. There is an omnipresent force in the universe that some call God, or the universal source, or simply source or higher consciousness. It doesn't matter what you call it, it's there for you too. We are not separate from higher consciousness; we are part of it, just as it is a part of us.

I've explored this notion of unity and connection throughout my life. I've written extensively about spirituality and personal development. I speak to groups on these topics. More importantly, I try to live with the principles and practices I've learned – the ones I share with you in this book.

When you are on the path to enlightenment, the ups and downs of life become easier to traverse. You will be healthier and less stressed. You will feel centred and self-aware, and more loving. That is a great way to live and, for that reason alone, it's worth learning about spirituality and adopting practices that will support your experience.

I hope this book will help and support you as you embark on your own spiritual exploration.

Polly Campbell, 2012

1

Starting on the path to enlightenment

In this chapter you will learn:

- ► *what spiritual enlightenment is*
- ► *how connecting with our spiritual side will lead to true fulfilment*
- ► *why the concept of enlightenment is relevant today*
- ► *the value of spiritual practice*
- ► *how to use this book.*

Self-assessment: How much do you know?

Answer the following questions to find out where you are now in your spiritual development.

1 A regular meditation practice requires:

   a An hour a day

   b At least a few minutes of quiet

   c A teacher to guide you

2 Gratitude is the simple practice of:

   a Writing thank-you notes for gifts you've received

   b Giving thanks for specific things in your life

   c Saying grace before dinner

3 To achieve the most benefit from guided imagery or visualization, you must be able to:

   a 'Picture' your life through images

   b Feel positive emotion

   c Listen to guided lessons on CD

4 Mindfulness is the practice of:

   a Thinking through solutions

   b Paying attention

   c Brainstorming

5 Regular meditation can:

   a Make you tired

   b Ease your pain

   c Improve your breathing

6 Diaphragmatic or belly breathing can:

   a Prevent hyperventilation

   b Diffuse stress

   c Clear your mind

7 Researchers say that those who regularly practise gratitude have:

  a Stronger bones

  b Higher immune function

  c More friends

8 If you give up resistance and accept things as they are, you will:

  a Get nothing done

  b Experience peace and clarity

  c Feel better, but be trapped by your bad choices

9 Your ego is:

  a The essence of who you are as an individual

  b An aspect of personality

  c The voice in your head that sounds like your cranky mother-in-law

10 Enlightenment is:

  a Something that can be experienced only by those who go on retreats, spend time in prayer and contemplation, and study with renowned teachers and yogis

  b An experience of awakening to higher consciousness so that we no longer experience separation from God

  c A religious experience

What did you discover?

If you selected mostly **b** answers, you have a good knowledge of the basic spiritual buzzwords and important practices that can help you live a more aware and connected life. If you came up with predominantly **a** and **c** answers, don't worry: this book will serve as a great introduction and guide to understanding these and other spiritual practices and principles.

The journey begins

Sit back, take a deep breath, and know that, simply by opening this book, you are embarking on a journey. This journey will spark your curiosity, ignite your passion and revitalize your life. Not only will it connect you to your radiant, authentic self but you will experience greater joy, deeper love and a developing faith.

> 'Enlightenment is having a mind that is open to everything while being attached to nothing.'
>
> Christopher Dorris, personal coach

During this process you will discover your true nature. You will see a self that is no longer ruled by ego or governed by limiting beliefs, a self that is no longer attached to expectations or external outcomes like money, promotions, compliments or social status, a self that feels alive and natural and in flow with the universe. It's there for you and it's worth exploring.

You will evolve spiritually as you study and complete the exercises in this book. To discover where you are now in your spiritual development, do the self-assessment quiz above. Don't fret if the concepts or ideas aren't familiar; you'll learn all you need to know in the pages to come, and the life experience that follows. In this book, we'll go deeper into the practices mentioned in the quiz and explore others *en route* to spiritual awakening.

As you'll discover, each of the practices is multi-dimensional and practical. Contrary to what many people think, spirituality can be broad and flexible in practice, as well as disciplined and focused. For example, a meditation practice can be worth while whether you do it for 5 or 50 minutes a day. Many of the traditions, such as mindfulness and gratitude, can be used anywhere and at any time.

By devoting some time each day to spiritual practice, you'll have an easier time integrating the habits and techniques that will help you live from your spiritual centre on a consistent basis.

Remember this

Feeling overwhelmed? Take a nature break. Go outside or look out of the window and notice the awe-inspiring landscape. Then consider this: the same source that created all this beauty created you too. You are part of it. It is part of you. You are not a product of your life's circumstance. You are a product of the highest, greatest energies in the universe.

Explaining enlightenment

Enlightenment is awakening. It is self-realization. It is consciousness.

There is no place you need to go, nothing you have to buy and nothing you have to do to improve to become enlightened – to become part of the universal source. By consciously aligning with your essence and spirit, you can live with the deep inner knowing that God is not a separate force, but the energy within you.

In this way, the state of enlightenment (which we discuss in greater detail in the next chapter) is not something to be obtained; it is something to be experienced. Even those of us who have not yet been enlightened have much to gain from regular spiritual practice and the personal growth that results from it.

Living separate from higher consciousness

Most of us struggle along the spiritual path because of our attachments and our ego-based beliefs. When you think that you must strive, aspire, produce or change to be worthy, you are actually distancing yourself from your spiritual essence.

Try it now

Sit quietly and say a little prayer. This can be in the form of a question, a statement of thanks or an expression of a hope or need. Say it aloud. Now sit quietly for a few minutes and ask yourself: 'What or who did I just pray to?' Allow your responses to flow intuitively. There are no wrong answers. Then contemplate this: the same omniscient power that heard your prayer also resides within you.

We've been taught that we must behave, follow the rules and live a certain way to be worthy of God's love. We've been conditioned to believe that we are separate from God: that God is something beyond us that both rewards and punishes.

Of course, none of that is true. We are not separate from universal consciousness: it is us. But we've forgotten who we are. Instead of working from spirit, then, we stay rooted in these limiting beliefs and ego-based ideas.

Key idea

When you are feeling stuck, bored, uncomfortable or dissatisfied, it could mean that you are operating from ego rather than your spiritual side. Spirit feels expansive. You feel connected to purpose. Everything else feels constrictive and narrow.

THE DISCONNECT THAT LEADS TO GLOBAL CRISIS

This isn't working well.

Our abundant planet is now facing widespread global crises because of the way we think and act, and the distance we've created between our selves and our spirituality. For centuries, we've subscribed to the belief that we are individuals who must fight, push and strive to get all that we need to survive. In response, we have created a culture that has overspent, overworked and overused our natural resources, our people and our energy in a massive attempt to get ahead, have more and become more powerful.

As a result, the international economy is failing, wars and violent attacks are rampant, animal species are endangered or extinct, and obesity and serious mental and physical health issues are endemic. More people than ever before are feeling undervalued, victimized, disenfranchised and stressed out. We are a global population living with sickness in body and spirit.

Remember this

The biggest problems we face cannot be solved solely from an intellectual perspective. Next time you encounter difficulty in your own life, approach it from a spiritual perspective. Ask yourself: 'What would Buddha or Jesus, or another one of the great masters, do?' Then act on that answer.

These things have occurred, in part, because we've moved away from our true nature. We have separated ourselves from our godliness and forgotten who we are. We have shut ourselves off from spirit. A society that believes success is achieved only through external reward cannot sustain itself. But one that operates with compassion, connection and consciousness can thrive.

Key idea

Compassion, kindness and tolerance are often the best responses to our most confounding challenges.

Waking up to a spiritual world

The good news is that we are not remaining unconscious. We have had it with the pain and poverty. We are tired of feeling stressed and overwhelmed and we are done with the mindset that tells us that, in order to be whole, we must disparage or defeat someone else.

As a culture, we are awakening to the knowledge that we cannot succeed, experience lasting love and joy or grow into our true purpose and potential when we see ourselves as separate from others and the energies that govern the universe.

This lingering feeling of disconnect that so many of us experience is prompting a spiritual evolution. We are looking for a better way and seeking a connection with higher consciousness. That search is leading us back towards our essential self.

Case study: Nancy

For Nancy, a 52-year-old retired advertising executive, living a spiritually based life is the one thing that has brought her happiness and a feeling of contentment, even during difficult times.

'Spirituality is not something separate that should only be considered on Sunday,' she says. 'It just goes hand in hand with how I'm supposed to – or at least try to – live my life.'

Nancy's own spiritual awareness began to shift when, as a young adult, she broke from the Catholic Church and began studying and learning about other religions and perspectives. After attending a lecture on loving kindness and Buddhism, Nancy began to live more in the moment and connect with her own personal happiness through compassion for others. Much of her spiritual work now is about becoming self-aware and open.

'There is no single right way to practise spirituality and no "right answer" when it comes to religion,' says Nancy. 'But I think you have to be honest with yourself and come to terms with how you live your life before you can grow spiritually. Identify the bad traits and work on them. Know that you might not be as important as you think you are. Understand that the person you are has a great effect on so many things in the universe. Take personal responsibility for being part of the good.'

Nancy says her greatest spiritual challenge now is to make time for further exploration and study. Yet aspects of our spirituality, like connection and compassion, are simply natural, she says.

'We're hardwired to have a connection with each other and to have compassion for each other. This is our true nature, and finding spirituality is a way to connect with that. The whole idea of finding true inner peace and personal happiness through connection to and compassion for others is a very powerful thought and it takes a sense of spirituality and contemplation to be a part of that.'

We are opening to the knowledge of a unified universe. We are seeking ways to connect with one another and our higher consciousness. Instead of pursuing our individual needs at the expense of others, more people are reaching out from kindness and compassion. Instead of bemoaning our lack, we are learning to be grateful for what we do have.

The world is waking up, becoming conscious to the fact that only when we align with our true nature will we feel most alive; only when we operate from love can we sustain our world; only when we live from source can we ease our suffering and awaken to our essence. We want peace, love and joy; and we are beginning to know that we already have all that, if only we rediscover our spirit.

Key idea

When we see ourselves as separate from universal consciousness, we behave as individuals, apart from all else. This disconnects us from our spiritual side and creates a life that ultimately feels unfulfilling, meaningless and lonely.

THE SOLUTIONS ARE SPIRITUAL

We can no longer find a quick fix for the troubles we're facing. There is no way to reason through these global challenges or individual tests. To search for intellectual solutions to the problems that seem to define our culture is to throw wood on a pyre: it only widens the gap of separation from self. When we spend time attempting to control, change, manipulate and manage external outcomes, we create greater distance from our spiritual self – the part that contains the insights and wisdom we seek.

ATTACHMENT TO THE IDEA OF ENLIGHTENMENT

It can be unsettling and even disappointing when we discover that we have separated from our true nature. That realization often compels us to find our way back. We want to experience unity, to live consciously, even though we are in the habit of living unconsciously. We are ready to learn a new way. We are ready to awaken. We desperately want the peace, joy and love that are promised to us when we do.

With this zealousness, we become attached to the idea of enlightenment and spirituality as a way out of our troubles. We become inspired by thoughts of our own awakening and we try to make it happen. Although it's enlightenment that we seek, in these early stages we often resort to our old intellectual and controlling habits to awaken. Spirituality becomes a goal rather than an experience.

Try it now

Read this entire visualization exercise. Then close your eyes and imagine it.

Imagine a bright, white light – pure energy – that starts in your heart centre and radiates throughout your body. It flows naturally through your organs, into your limbs and out through your fingers, toes and the top of your head. There is nothing you have to do but follow where this energy leads. It is from your highest source. Trust it and it will lead you to the insights you need to become conscious.

Remember this

You do not have to force your spirituality. You are already a spiritual being. You must simply become aware of it and operate more from spirit than intellect.

The value of spiritual practice

From this perspective, we are again operating from the doing, being and controlling dynamic of ego. We are attaching ourselves to the notion that we must manage or complete something in order to be spiritual. This mindset only adds to our stress and uncertainty and broadens our separation from source.

Enlightenment, though, is our natural state; we simply need to establish habits that help us to return to the essence of who we are. This takes practice, but it is not one of desperation or drudgery.

Spiritual practice is sparked more by curiosity, openness and a sincere desire to know ourselves better and to live more authentically. The habits we form help us develop our awareness. Then we can nourish our spiritual nature until it radiates through all that we do.

This shift in awareness doesn't guarantee a blissful state. Nor is the process of awakening always comfortable. It can be disorienting and confusing as you shed your outer skin for the inner being. But it is also honest and liberating. It is a way to live with joy and love and truth, even when the circumstances in your daily life appear complex and confusing.

Key idea

Spiritual growth and development are a direct result of active living. If you integrate, practise and contemplate these and other spiritual insights and techniques, you will experience a shift in consciousness. This is not a passive process – it is a way of engaging in life.

Moving into the light

Imagine that you've spent your whole life in a dark room and you are now curious about what it looks like: the colour of the walls and where the bed sits. First you light a candle and see the pattern on the duvet. You notice, too, the beautiful shadows dancing along the ceiling. They create some distortion and some illusion, but you trust that the view will become clearer as you continue to turn on the lights. You are uncertain about what you'll find, but excited by the possibility of all that is there.

Next, you open the blinds and let a little more light in. You see the details in the mouldings and the portrait on the wall. Finally, you turn on the light switch and everything – from the cobwebs in the corner to the blue paint on the door – becomes clear and obvious. You see it all: the scuffs in the wood floor, the carvings in the headboard, the design on the ceiling. It's all visible and it's all fine just as it is. In fact, you are grateful and buoyant that you are finally getting a clear look.

This is how enlightenment works. With spiritual practice and attention, you will move through the stages of awakening until the lights go on in your life. This is helpful to the rest of us. When you are living an authentic and spiritual life, you inspire others to move through their own darkness and into the light.

Remember this

Next time you're feeling out of sorts or stressed, take time before lashing out simply to notice your emotions. Awareness is essential to awakening and often, by becoming aware of your experience and feelings, you'll be able to diffuse the energy of bad feelings and make a more conscious response.

How this book can help

In these pages, you'll learn practices and strategies that will guide you along this path. You will acquire information that will help you establish your own habits and experience spiritual growth. You will also pick up some knowledge about ego and the other barriers that keep us unconscious and disconnected.

Each chapter includes quizzes to help you determine where you are in your spiritual process, as well as tips and exercises like the 'Try it now' features designed to support your awakening through regular daily and in-the-moment practices. The 'Remember this' sections in each chapter offer practical techniques that can help you stay connected to spirit any time, anywhere. The case studies illustrate how others integrate a daily spiritual practice into their own lives.

STEP-BY-STEP OR STRAIGHT THROUGH

There is no right or wrong way to read this book or use the information or exercises presented here. It is a guide to support you whenever and however you need. But, just as living a spiritually based life is an active process, you'll be best served if you take an active role in learning, practising and applying the concepts on these pages. In other words, you are likely to see more growth if you do the exercises.

In the beginning, you may want to read the book straight through and then reread resonant chapters and sections to learn better how to adapt the information for your own use. You may choose to go chapter by chapter, giving time to each exercise. Find what works for you, but commit to the process.

Don't get caught up in judgment while reading. Try to suspend your doubts and simply allow the information in. While this book will be an impetus for spiritual growth, your greatest lessons will come through direct experience.

If this book inspires you to try new things, to seek greater knowledge, to establish supportive practices, follow that inspiration. Get curious. Become aware. Be open and watch what life serves up as you begin on your own path to awakening.

JOURNAL TO UNDERSTANDING

You may find it helpful to keep a journal while you read this book and then throughout your spiritual journey. Use it to capture thoughts and questions while you read, or to record the answers to the quizzes or your experiences with the exercises. Use it at the end of each day to record your thoughts, feelings and frustrations as your awareness begins to shift.

Keeping a journal helps ease stress and contributes to health and clarity, and it is just one more way to integrate what you learn with how you live.

Try it now

Open your journal and for five minutes write about why you are reading this book and what you hope to learn. Don't edit or worry about grammar or punctuation; just clarify your goals and what you hope to gain from the experience. Knowing what we desire is the start of allowing it in.

CENTURIES OF INSIGHT AND KNOWLEDGE

Many of the strategies and principles covered in this book have been around for thousands of years. The great masters, like Buddha, Jesus and Krishna, taught these principles, and they are just as relevant today as they were then.

We cannot live a joy-filled, whole life when we are disconnected from the most powerful part of ourselves – our higher consciousness. We cannot solve the problems of the world when we are seeking only an intellectual solution. We cannot fulfil our divine purpose when we are separate from our divinity.

We can, however, begin a spiritual exploration that will awaken us to the higher energies of the universe. We do not have to remain separate any longer. We can be free of the fears and beliefs and external scaffolding that teach us that we need to work and strive to become our best selves.

We can begin this journey to wholeness, this process of healing, right now, by becoming aware – by awakening to the idea that there is more to life than what we can see.

Focus points

✻ Enlightenment is when we awaken to our true nature and realize that we are a part of source energy or higher consciousness.

✻ Living a spiritual life helps us gain the awareness needed to awaken.

✻ The greatest problems we have are a result of our belief that we must work, strive, fight and achieve as individuals to be successful.

✻ When we realize our power as divine energy, not only will we feel better in our lives, but we will make a positive contribution to the world.

✻ This book introduces some of the key spiritual principles and practices that will help you in your journey of spiritual growth.

Next step

When we understand that we are spiritual beings connected to – not separate from – source, we can begin our journey towards awakening. Throughout this book you'll have a chance to do exercises and learn specific practices that will help you awaken to this insight. In the next chapter, we'll go deeper into the concept of enlightenment and explore the different stages of enlightenment.

2

Defining enlightenment

In this chapter you will learn:

- ▸ *different definitions of enlightenment*
- ▸ *how some of the world's major religions view enlightenment*
- ▸ *the difference between the Age of Enlightenment and spiritual enlightenment*
- ▸ *how we experience moments of awakening*
- ▸ *how spirituality contributes to enlightenment.*

Self assessment: What are your beliefs about spirituality?

Answer true or false to the following questions to determine how open and ready you are to pursue a path of spiritual growth.

1 You believe things happen for a reason.   T/F

2 You have much to be grateful for.   T/F

3 You worry that, if you accept things as they are, you will   T/F
become lazy and complacent.

4 Spirituality requires you to have a religious background.   T/F

5 There is a universal force that is greater than what you   T/F
can see.

6 Life is filled with rules and requirements that you must   T/F
follow to be successful.

7 You believe that your life has meaning and purpose.   T/F

8 You're interested in a spiritual practice but you don't have   T/F
the time to do it.

9 You've tried meditating and you can't do it right, so there's   T/F
no reason to continue.

10 You are a naturally curious person.   T/F

What did you discover?

If you answered 'true' to questions 1, 2, 5, 7 and 10, you are ready to begin a spiritual exploration that includes further self-inquiry and devoted spiritual practice. You will face challenges and uncertainty, since spiritual exploration requires you to meet your limiting beliefs and peel away long-held views and habits that no longer serve you, but this is also a time of exhilaration and expansion.

If you answered 'true' to questions 3, 4, 6, 8 and 9, you may be mired in some resistance about spirituality and what a spiritual practice requires. That's good to know about yourself. Often, we are unaware of the areas of resistance that limit our experience. Now you have a chance to examine yours.

Enlightenment is an experience

Awakening. Self-realization. Consciousness.

These words – and others – have been used to define
enlightenment. Some think of it as a state to pursue, a place
to reach or an outcome – nirvana. To others it is a lifestyle,
a way of being in the world, one that emerges after spiritual
exploration, and the transcendence of earthly suffering and
limitation.

Today, as the global consciousness shifts to a more openly
spiritual perspective, enlightenment is understood as a natural
state of consciousness. You don't have to be a monk, a mystic,
a guru or a yogi to experience this kind of awakening. It can
occur in a flash and last a brief moment through a spark of
insight or awareness, or it can be a consistent way of living
in this world, one rooted in peace, self-knowledge and an
awareness of God.

UNDERSTANDING BEGINS WITH INQUIRY

Enlightenment can evolve through a natural progression of
spiritual study and growth. For Buddha, it came after years of
meditation. Whether we become enlightened or not, there is
much to learn, experience and enjoy along the spiritual path. All
spiritual development begins with a process of self-inquiry and
a willingness to suspend what we think we know for a more
open-minded approach to life.

Resistance touches all of us at some time or another, but
spiritual practice can help us transform our resistance into
peace and acceptance. That topic will be the primary focus of
the next chapter. For now, try to suspend your resistance just
long enough to keep reading. You will find that the strategies
contained in this book will support your spiritual growth,
help you gain self-knowledge, inspire peace of mind and
offer the possibility that you too can awaken to your greatest
potential.

Key idea

'In a single moment, in one stroke, you can become enlightened. It is not a gradual process, because enlightenment is not something that you have to invent. It is something that you have to discover. It is already there. It is not something that you have to manufacture. If you have to manufacture it, of course, it will take time; but it is already there. Close your eyes and see it there. Be silent and have a taste of it. Your very nature is what I call enlightenment. Enlightenment is not something alien, outside you. It is not somewhere else in time and space. It is you, your very core.'

Osho

Remember this

You don't need to have right answers or an intellectual understanding of enlightenment to become enlightened. However, you must be willing to engage in life, open your mind to new insights, pay attention, and be still in the emptiness that comes when what you thought you knew falls away.

The enlightened self

To truly awaken, to be enlightened, means you no longer fret or manage or control or worry about the state of the world, because you know deeply that the world is okay just as it is. There is no longer any need to judge or manipulate. There is no place to go, nothing that needs to be fixed, or hidden, or achieved. In this expanded, awakened state, we see our limitations, but we know them not as limitations, because we are no longer attached to outcomes or judgment. We simply experience all that is from a place of wonder and peace and love.

This new way of experiencing life can be disorienting, unsettling and even uncomfortable for a time. We are more familiar with doing. We like to be busy working to achieve some external mark of success and social status. We are more comfortable searching for answers to our every question than settling with what we know intuitively.

We are not in the habit of letting things be. We don't like uncertainty. We are not used to going within to discover that God is already there and that all the answers we need are there too. Yet this is the wisdom, the knowing, that is there to be discovered through spiritual practice and awakening.

> 'Awakening is an end of seeking and a beginning to who you really are.'

> Adyashanti, spiritual teacher and author

WE ARE BIGGER THAN THE ROLES WE PLAY

Any explanation of enlightenment will fall short, because enlightenment can be known truly only through experience. It cannot be easily defined or taught, and no word is big enough to express the expansiveness of this state. To know what awakening is is to be awakened. That starts with self-inquiry.

Try it now

Sit quietly, feet on the floor, hands in your lap or on the arms of a chair, and ask this question: 'Who am I?' Then be open to the ideas – whatever they are – that come. When the thoughts stop, continue by asking, 'How do I know?' Listen again for the answers. Write in your journal about the experience.

WHO AM I?

We usually define ourselves by the roles we play, our physical appearance and the jobs we do. We are the lawyer or the teacher, the mother or the husband. We are young or old, fat or thin. But, we are so much more than the labels we wear in life.

As we awaken, we begin to see the truth of who we really are. We begin to connect to our essential spirit, the creative force and energy that animate and flow through us. Self-inquiry and spiritual practice help us become conscious of this knowledge that we are bigger than what we see, or believe, or know.

Case study: Paul

Each morning Paul begins the day in personal reflection. Inquiry and contemplation are a major aspect of his spirituality, which has shifted as his life has shifted and changed over the decades.

Paul, a writer and former seminarian, began to question many of the religious and spiritual ideas he'd grown up with. He left the seminary to marry and also, after years of questioning and study, discovered the Unitarian-universalist church. Here he found a tradition that encourages study, contemplation and wonder – all of which he integrates into his morning reflections. He also uses this morning time to meditate on theological beliefs.

Paul says that spirituality provides the 'centre' for his life but admits that it can be difficult to maintain faith in a tumultuous world. Through spiritual practice he's found 'greater compassion for others as well as an acceptance and appreciation of the growing and diverse human society'.

Spiritual exploration has also helped Paul to cultivate a greater sense of patience – with himself and others. 'It allows me to confront and learn from my own strengths and weaknesses,' he says. And during the tough times, he remembers a basic principle common to almost all spiritual practice: 'All things are fleeting.'

Age-old practices ignite spiritual exploration

This process of spiritual exploration and growth is fulfilling, interesting and worth while, whether or not you ever reach the desired 'state of enlightenment'. There is much to be gained by adopting habits and practices that can help you understand yourself better, love more and connect to each living thing with kindness and compassion. When we live a spiritual life, we experience greater peace and genuine joy as we gradually move through the stages of awakening.

Though we may be learning these practices for the first time, the ideas are centuries old. As already mentioned, they have been taught, practised, preached and written about by the great philosophers and spiritual masters and within the world's largest religions.

Key idea

Enlightenment is a deep awareness of our essence – our spirit. It is not something to be attained or a goal to be achieved. In many ways, it is the natural evolution of our spiritual practice and self-awareness that leads to a shift in consciousness and the knowledge that we are one with God.

Religious traditions, from the monotheistic faiths of Judaism, Christianity and Islam to the eastern teachings of Buddhism and Hinduism, have all contributed insight and perspective to the understanding of spiritual enlightenment. Religion, after all, emerged to help people awaken to their faith and move into the higher consciousness that is God.

HINDUISM AND ENLIGHTENMENT

For Hindus, one of the four ultimate purposes in life is *moksha*, or enlightenment. Enlightenment in Hinduism means an end to reincarnation, and therefore an end to the earthly suffering that plagues unenlightened souls. This end of suffering comes from the deep knowledge and clarity of the truth that is God: that God is all and fully self-realized.

ENLIGHTENMENT AND BUDDHISM

The term enlightenment is most often associated with Buddhism, named for Siddhartha Gautama who became the Buddha, or Enlightened One, after discovering the path to enlightenment through meditation.

Buddhism speaks of the Sanskrit word *bodhi*, a term meaning freedom from suffering and ignorance. It can also be translated to mean 'awakening' and it is often thought to be synonymous with nirvana, that peaceful state that comes when you are liberated from suffering and therefore enlightened.

In Zen Buddhism, enlightenment is available to anyone after much spiritual practice. An individual on the spiritual path may experience *kensho*, a brief, unique experience of enlightenment, and *satori*, a sudden flash of insight yielding deep awareness, knowledge and awakening like that experienced by Buddha and other masters. *Satori* implies a transformational experience of awakening, according to *The Concise Oxford Dictionary of World Religions* by John Bowker.

Both Buddhism and Hinduism describe 'enlightenment' (or a Sanskrit equivalent) as the culmination of a long and solitary process of personal reflection and contemplation. The nature of both these traditions as 'free faiths' eliminates the need to adhere to a predetermined doctrine, or creed, as a prerequisite for achieving the highest level of consciousness, which is a oneness with all spiritual reality and the final triumph over the temporal world.

JUDAISM AND ENLIGHTENMENT

In Judaism, the awakened state is sometimes called *devekut*, or 'communion with God'. This enlightenment is the knowledge resulting from a prolonged period of thought and reflection on the presence of God in our lives, and not on the nature of God himself, which remains enshrouded in mystery. This is accomplished through the study of and meditation on the evolving body of Jewish literature: the Torah, the Midrash and the Kabbalah texts.

Jewish mystics who practise Kabbalah sometimes equate *devekut* with ecstasy. Kabbalists believe that an individual's soul has three aspects. One part is completed at physical birth but the other two evolve only through the experiences, actions and beliefs adopted by the individual. Each of the three parts of the soul is fully developed only in people who are awakened and enlightened.

ENLIGHTENMENT AND CHRISTIANITY

Historically, some leaders of Christian churches have been repelled by the idea of enlightenment, as it is so often associated with the eastern philosophies of Hinduism and Buddhism. However, many of the teachings of Jesus and his disciples speak of the concept of humans' unity with God, a major aspect of enlightenment in most religious traditions. For example, John's Gospel (17:22–4) says: 'I have given them the glory that you gave me, that they may be one as we are one: I in them and you in me.'

Christian enlightenment is concerned mostly with the individual's intimate (or mystical) meeting or communion with God, who remains an entirely separate entity. As such, Christian enlightenment takes on a different ontology from Eastern traditions, and can exist only within the creeds of traditional Christianity. Enlightenment can occur only through Jesus as a mediator, and it will ultimately result in eternal life after death.

Bernard McGinn, theologian and scholar of Western mysticism, defines Christian mysticism as a form of spirituality that 'concerns the preparation for, the consciousness of, and the reaction to...the immediate or direct presence of God'.

Christian mystics themselves spend much time in disciplined spiritual practice, prayer and contemplation – practices long thought to be necessary to awakening – and they are generally considered to be people who develop the intimate, unified relationship with God necessary for enlightenment.

SUFISM AND ENLIGHTENMENT
Bawa Muhaiyaddeen, a Sufi mystic and teacher, once described Sufism, a mystical sect of the Islamic religion, as *La illaha Il Allahu,* which may be translated to mean, 'Nothing other than God exists. You alone are God.' He explains that Sufism is the deep knowing that the self no longer exists. Only God remains. When you awaken into this knowing of a unified universe, you are enlightened.

Through knowledge and discipline, Sufis seek 'a direct understanding and experience of God', according to Paul Oliver in his book *World Faiths – An Introduction* (Teach Yourself, 2010).

Try it now

Write in your journal what you believe are your 'Rules for life'.

* What beliefs do you hold about the things that must happen for you to be fulfilled or successful?
* What is your moral conduct?
* What is important to you?
* What makes life meaningful?

Allow the words to tumble out in a stream-of-consciousness style. Don't worry about grammar or punctuation; allow the thought and feeling to emerge on the page. Then take a look at what you wrote and ask these two questions: 'Can I give all of that up?' 'Can I open to the possibility that there is more to life than what I see here?' Contemplate your answers.

Remember this

Pause for a moment and consider your religious background. How did it influence your view of God, your connection to a divine source, and any thoughts about who can or cannot reach an enlightened state? You don't have to judge those thoughts. Simply become aware of what they are. Know, too, that enlightenment is there for each of us — no matter what our background.

The Age of Enlightenment versus spiritual enlightenment

While early religious leaders and spiritual seekers were pondering (and often enforcing with a heavy hand) the role of religion and spirituality in daily life, the 17th and 18th centuries in Europe were defined by another kind of awakening. This period, known as the Age of Enlightenment, was marked by an intellectual and cultural shift.

For the first time, scientists, philosophers and scholars sought to understand the world and humanity through reason, study and inquiry rather than through religion and metaphysics. They challenged church doctrines, eschewed long-held traditions, debunked superstitions and scrutinized philosophical beliefs. This was a period of intellectual, not spiritual, inquiry, a period of scientific awakening rather than an awakening to higher consciousness. One of the outcomes was a fracture between faith-based knowledge and rational thought.

ENLIGHTENMENT IS SPIRITUAL, NOT RELIGIOUS
Today, knowledge of self and God is essential to any discussion of spiritual enlightenment. While the major religions do direct us to awaken to God's presence and live in truth and love as opposed to judgment and suffering, enlightenment is a decidedly spiritual experience. It is not limited to a specific philosophical view, religious perspective or definition of God.

Try it now

You are not defined or limited by the events of your life. With awareness, you can cast off the labels and limitations that are keeping you separate from self-realization.

Sit still, feet flat on the floor. Take a deep breath and, for one minute, just focus on the feelings in your body. Do not judge or define them; just experience them. Connecting to the body is one way to get out of the ruminating thoughts of the mind and start building the awareness that you are more than merely a physical being.

Key idea

No religious background is required for spiritual development. While each of the world's largest religious groups follows specific doctrines and teachings, most of them also address the importance of self-knowledge and unity with God. Those aspects are also the purpose of spiritual practice and development.

Starting from darkness

The process of awakening begins when you start to question who you are and the purpose of your very existence. You might start by asking, 'Is this all there is?' or, 'Who am I?'

Until we begin questioning, we are unconscious. We are vague about anything beyond ourselves. We produce, work, succeed and fail, all the while believing that physical and material merits and outcomes are a measure of our own worth and value.

In this place of unconsciousness, we believe, too, that we can control circumstances and people to get what we want and need. Our ego reigns supreme here, filling us with unchallenged thoughts and beliefs and fears about our lack of worthiness, or righteousness. We are deeply connected to our ego and our individualism. God exists only as something separate, out there.

Ultimately, this leaves us feeling restless, insecure and unhappy. We look around, trying to find ways to soothe ourselves. Perhaps we drink, shop, eat, complain or just remain stuck in unfulfilling patterns and bad habits.

This dissatisfaction can also prompt us to start looking more closely at what we think we know. For the first time, we consider the notion that there might be something else. This is usually when the first glimmer of light appears.

What happens next in the process is described in dozens of different ways. Some spiritual writers and teachers claim there are three stages, others say five, eight or even eleven. But, one thing is clear: spiritual growth and awakening are unique and profound for every individual, yet supported by all who have awakened before.

Key idea

Hundreds of books, articles and religious documents offer different perspectives on enlightenment and the stages you must pass through to experience what Buddhists refer to as a state of nirvana. The core concept is consistent in all of them: you move from a state of unconsciousness, or darkness, into the light of self-realization, God or source energy.

No matter how you traverse your path or delineate the stages you encounter along the way, three distinct things are going to happen as you experience self-actualization:

- you will become more aware
- you will sense a universal connection to all
- you will know God.

THREE STAGES OF ENLIGHTENMENT
1 Becoming aware of life as it is

It may happen suddenly or be a gradual experience but, at some point, spiritual exploration starts with the knowledge that there is something beyond the job and the house and the fancy car. There is some bigger, guiding force in your life and you start to become curious about what that is.

In this stage, you become present to the moments of your life and the possibility of a higher consciousness. You begin to see yourself as a part of the world instead of apart from it. This prompts self-inquiry, contemplation and study. You ask big questions like: 'Who am I?' 'What is my purpose?' 'What else is there?' And you search for understanding. Greater meaning emerges from the life you are living, and yet you are still connected to the physical realm and your familiar habits. This can sometimes feel frustrating and it can be difficult to merge your dawning spirituality with your existing lifestyle.

2 Connecting to all that is

At some point, this self-inquiry expands from the intellectual knowledge of a higher consciousness into a direct connection with it. You begin to lead from your heart and trust your intuition a little more. You become more aware of your emotions. Instead of seeing others as separate, you have awakened now to the knowledge that what you do affects others, even a world away. You see – in a very real way – how everything is connected by energy.

Now you know that your life has purpose and so do the lives of all whom you encounter. You practise gratitude and compassion and you know that the challenges faced by others are the challenges you will also face. You are inspired to live from the higher energies of love and inspiration and you begin to know through a greater consciousness that everything – even the most difficult moments – is here to serve you. And all offer opportunity for awakening. Through spiritual practice, your faith begins to flourish and you deepen your connection to God and to self.

3 Living with God

You are spirit. It is you. God is both within you and outside you. You don't need to talk about it or prove it. You know it. In this stage, you feel at peace. You live in the present moment. This is what many call enlightenment.

This is liberating because you no longer feel limited by your physical body or beliefs. You are no longer attached to external roles and rewards. You aren't afraid. There is no need to control or manipulate to get ahead. From here, you can watch the world without trying to change it. You are fully self-aware, fully conscious, and living from your highest self, radiating peace and love. This stage is literally described as 'becoming one with the light'.

AWAKENING IN THE MOMENT

Long before you reach a place of total enlightenment, it's likely that you will have moments of awakening. In these moments, all your senses seem heightened and you are infused with awareness and clarity. The world appears more vibrant and beautiful, and peace and serenity pervade everything.

Researcher and author Steven Taylor writes of it this way: 'We feel serene and whole inside, and our normal problems and worries seem to fade into insignificance. The world seems like a benevolent and meaningful place, and we feel part of everything around us, with an intense empathic connection with other people.'

These awakening moments most often occur when our usually limited and narrow awareness of the world falls away, leaving a broader view. This can happen when you experience awe or inspiration. Natural landscapes or environmental marvels such as pristine mountain peaks or stormy, crashing waves can evoke these emotions. Moments of awakening can also occur during meditation or even while listening to powerful, moving music.

Try it now

Turn on your favourite music. For five minutes, sit with your eyes closed and soak in the sounds.

Tapping into the beauty that surrounds us yields to inspiration. Inspiration reminds us that there is more to life than what we can intellectually understand. When you experience this insight, the light is coming on.

Remember this

Regular spiritual practice can help us develop greater awareness and insight. Practices such as mindfulness, meditation and visualization (discussed in the chapters to come) do, in fact, get easier with repetition. Schedule time each day for spiritual practice, as you would regular exercise, and build it into your life.

Benefits of a spiritual path

These brief moments of awakening offer glimpses of what life can be like all the time if we live a spiritual life and align with source energy. These moments illuminate for us the beauty and the energy and the love that is all around us, if only we become conscious.

Aside from the knowledge, peace and bliss that people are said to experience when they shift into this higher consciousness, the practices that we use to get there – like mindfulness, meditation and visualization – can, in their own way, make our day-to-day life more satisfying and pleasant.

Some of the benefits of spiritual practice include:

► lower blood pressure

► better immune function

► lower stress levels

► greater wellbeing

► healthier relationships.

These provide some compelling reasons to begin our own spiritual exploration.

Key idea

Spiritual growth does not depend on reaching an enlightened state. In fact, the process of self-discovery and awareness, the process of awakening to the truth of life, is revealing and expansive and healthy in its own right. Each moment of life – including the challenges and hardships – presents an opportunity for development. You have not failed if you are not yet enlightened. You have expanded because of your practice.

Focus points

✳ Enlightenment is also referred to as awakening, self-realization, higher consciousness or self-actualization.

✳ Spiritual enlightenment involves a shift in consciousness from the ego-based self to the awareness that we are all connected and all one. We are no longer separate from God.

✳ Spiritual practices, such as prayer, mindfulness and meditation, help us achieve a shift in consciousness.

✳ Doctrines from most major world religions talk about unity with the divine and the importance of self-knowledge.

✳ Engaging in spiritual practice also provides profound physical and emotional benefits including better immune system function, less stress and greater wellbeing.

Next step

Spiritual practice not only leads us towards a deeper awareness of God but also helps us live happier, healthier lives in the process. Practices such as meditation, mindfulness and gratitude foster peace and compassion and help us overcome self-imposed barriers. In the next chapter we'll explore these benefits and barriers as we learn to develop our own spiritual practice.

3

Beginning your spiritual practice

In this chapter you will learn:

- ► *the difference between knowledge and experiential enlightenment*
- ► *how to examine the limiting beliefs about ourselves that can stand in the way of enlightenment*
- ► *the benefits of and barriers to spiritual practice*
- ► *how to establish a spiritual practice.*

Self-assessment: What is your spiritual mindset?

Establishing a spiritual practice starts by creating an environment and attitude that are conducive to growth. Answer true or false to the following questions to identify the things you can do – or might already be doing – to support your spiritual life.

1. You are comfortable sitting quietly, alone with your thoughts. **T/F**
2. You recognize that spiritual growth requires dedication, practice and attention. **T/F**
3. You believe that there is more to life than what you can see and express through your five senses. **T/F**
4. You are more interested in discovering the peace of enlightenment than establishing a spiritual practice. **T/F**
5. You are willing to consider different perspectives and opinions. **T/F**
6. In order to learn spiritual concepts, you believe that you must have a teacher or yogi. **T/F**
7. You direct kindness and compassion at yourself even when you make mistakes. **T/F**
8. You spend a few moments in conscious reflection each day. **T/F**
9. In your home, you have a specific place that feels peaceful and comfortable. **T/F**
10. There is a 'right' way to apply these practices and, when you work out how, awareness becomes easy. **T/F**

What did you discover?

If you answered 'true' to every question except for numbers 4, 6 and 10, you are indeed creating an environment conducive to spiritual growth. The goal is not to reach a state of enlightenment and then be finished with the process; it is to create a fully aware and meaningful life experience along the way.

Remember this

Connecting to your spiritual side starts with a choice. You can choose to approach this process of spiritual growth with openness and curiosity. Once you do that, spirituality becomes a natural path.

Spiritual schools of thought

Plenty of experts, gurus and teachers can guide you in spiritual practice. Many of them are wise, kind and insightful people. While working with a teacher can fuel rapid growth and deeper understanding, you have still got to do the practice, study and contemplation. Nobody can make you more spiritual; it is something you must decide to do for yourself.

Some teachers talk in absolutes; they operate from a particular perspective, with a narrow viewpoint about exactly how awakening can be achieved. They believe that if you follow certain steps and rules, then *voilà*, you are enlightened! Not so fast!

True awakening is the dissolution of all that. It's a shift in perception that leads to the letting go of what we think we know in favour of inquiry and acceptance. It's a release from the limitations of ego and the suffering that comes from our attachment to ideas and beliefs and objects and things.

When we awaken, we step into the awareness that we are infinite, spiritual beings. This doesn't mean that every moment is easy and blissful. As spiritual teacher Adyashanti says, this transition to greater awareness can be 'disorienting'. If, instead of hiding from the experience, we become present to it – willing to engage and question what we think we know – this will lead us to a greater sense of peace and authenticity. It also allows us to embrace and love the moments of our life.

This is our natural state, the one that arrives when we give up the stories, opinions, judgments, habits and conditions that have been embedded in us since birth. When we can release the idea of who we think we ought to be, we become more of who we truly are – spiritual beings infused with light, compassion, love and joy.

Spiritual practice, then, is used to lead us back to our true nature and essence. It helps us rediscover who we are and reminds us who we have always been, so that we can live more often from that conscious place.

'The goal of spiritual practice', writes Rabbi Alan Lurie, 'is to help us see that we are more than temporary and meaningless collections of automatic emotional and physical responses. All spiritual practices are designed to lead us to see a higher reality – that we are, in truth, eternal consciousness, occupying a physical form for a purpose, animated and connected to the creative and sustaining source of everything. Spirituality is, in essence, the experience of waking up to this higher, truer reality.'

Remember this

Spend less time thinking about the different theories and practices and more time living the spiritual principles of gratitude, compassion, love and joy. Contemplate one of those qualities today and begin to notice how it shows in your life.

How experience impacts enlightenment

Experiential theory says that our habits, attitudes, beliefs and conditioned responses are the sum of our life experiences and, in many ways, a barrier to enlightenment. In order to awaken, we must disconnect from the habits and conditioned responses that keep us separate from spirit. We must rid ourselves of judgment, attachment and other behaviour that usually come up around our physical appearance, our finances and our relationships. Any belief that causes us to feel unworthy or inadequate is false and serves only to keep us stuck, reactive and frustrated.

Here are some of the limiting beliefs that trap people:

▶ I'm not smart enough.

▶ I don't have enough money.

▶ I'm not talented enough to make a difference.

- My body isn't strong enough.
- I don't deserve anything better.
- I'm unlovable.
- There's nothing I can do to change things.
- I don't have the time.
- I have no choice.
- I'll never amount to anything else.
- It's always my fault.
- I can't lose weight no matter how hard I try.

Often, these kinds of negative beliefs and thought patterns prompt people to begin spiritual exploration in the first place. After experiencing great pain or hardship as a result of conditioned beliefs and behaviour, many people start looking for other options. They are desperate to leave the pain and trouble behind and are willing to begin the process of self-inquiry in an effort to awaken to something better or to at least ascribe meaning to the troubling times.

The way to awaken from these unconscious attitudes and beliefs, according to experiential theory, is to liberate ourselves from those conditioned responses. This can be done through spiritual practice and study, therapy, hypnosis and other clearing methods. It can also occur when we recognize our own unity with source.

Understanding knowledge theory

Knowledge theory describes those who simply awaken to the deep knowledge and understanding that they are unified with God.

The knowledge theory of enlightenment, writes James Swartz, is the 'settled conviction, based on direct observation, that there is only one self, the nature of which is ever-free consciousness, or awareness, and that I am it.'

This removes the ego. It removes our limiting beliefs and the conditioned responses that cause us to feel imperfect or incomplete. When we become infused with the self-realization that God is within and without, our attachments fall away, our fears dissipate, and we stop striving and begin being. We are no longer required to remove our limitations, because there are none.

It's important, however, to be cautious of clinging too tightly to models and theories or practices. Any attachment to the idea of awakening will move you further from it.

While both knowledge and experiential theories are valid ways for us to think about this experience of enlightenment, no description is completely adequate. The only way truly to understand awakening is through direct knowing. Awakening is known by the heart and soul, not through the rational mind. It can be experienced within any moment without effort, as well as after years of study, practice and self-inquiry.

Try it now

Conditioned responses and limiting beliefs impact every part of our lives. Complete this exercise in your journal and begin to notice how your conditioned responses appear in your life.

1 Pick one physical attribute that you don't like.
2 Explain why you don't like it.
3 Now answer these questions:
   a Is it possible that you don't like this feature because someone else criticized it?
   b Is it possible that you are comparing your attribute to an image of what you think you 'ought' to look like?
   c Can you let go of this idea or repetitive thought pattern and replace it with acceptance?

This kind of self-inquiry can help tease out the limiting and false beliefs that are operating in your life. Try this exercise with anything in your life that seems lacking – relationships, financial situations, jobs or health, for example. By becoming aware of what your limiting beliefs are, you diffuse their power.

Remember this

Spend a few minutes each day becoming aware of what you're thinking. When you can recognize that your thoughts aren't necessarily true, you can begin to challenge thoughts that feel limiting. Discard those that aren't loving, kind, peaceful, or otherwise connected to the higher energies of your spirit. You don't have to believe everything you think.

Key idea

Different theories and approaches are used to describe and support our enlightenment but, no matter how it's defined, it is available to anyone at any time.

LIVING YOUR BEST LIFE

Our task, then, is to think less of our own enlightenment and to focus on living our best life. We need to adopt principles and habits that will aid us, teach us and help us connect to the light within. By living closer to spirit during the routines of our daily lives, we will feel greater peace, love and joy. Our task is to become conscious to the lives we are living and to trust that we will discover all we need to know to buoy our own awakening. Daily spiritual practice can help us in that discovery process.

Key idea

Spiritual practice is not separate from the circumstances of our daily lives. We can always act with compassion, operate from love, and live with awareness. Regular daily practice of these skills and principles can make it easier to connect to our spiritual self in any moment.

BECOMING CURIOUS AND OPEN

You don't have to achieve enlightenment to make spiritual practice worth while. Nor do you have to quit your job, invest in a mountain retreat or move to India. Opportunities for spiritual growth happen all along the way, if you're paying attention. Yet most of us get caught up in the stress of our daily lives. We get stuck in judgments and opinions and focus more on how to get what we want, rather than how we can learn from our experience.

This is a narrow approach. We gravitate towards things that are easy to define, and we label circumstances as good or bad, black or white, right or wrong. We become reactive rather than curious. When you try new things, stay open to different possibilities and pay attention to the process rather than the outcome. By doing so, your spiritual awareness will also expand. By openly engaging in life, you will see clearly that everything is here to help us become more conscious.

Try it now

Stop what you are doing and for three minutes look at an object nearby – something that is part of your regular environment such as a coffee cup, a candlestick, a mobile phone or a light switch. Really study it. Touch it, use all your senses to 'see' this thing that you use every day. Challenge yourself to find something about it that you've never noticed before. Spiritual connection begins with curiosity, by noticing and experiencing what has been there all along.

THE POWER OF SPIRITUAL PRACTICE

Many of us have long been unconscious to our spiritual selves. Now, as we reawaken, we need to form habits and practices to support that reconnection. As when we acquire any new habit, the more we act as spiritual beings, the easier it becomes to live authentically from our spiritual core. This is worth doing – whether we become enlightened or not – because when we live true to our essence, we feel better and we make positive contributions to the world.

Here are some of the other benefits researchers now know evolve from an established spiritual practice:

▶ Gratitude improves overall wellbeing, boosts mood and eases depression.

▶ Meditation can ease the perception of pain and stress.

▶ Mindfulness lowers stress, blood pressure and heart rate, and it reduces anxiety.

- Prayer has been shown to aid in forgiveness, and forgiveness promotes wellbeing.

- Compassion improves immune function.

- Self-compassion boosts productivity and accountability.

- Positive contribution and generosity can help you live longer.

- Many of the practices enhance focus and concentration.

Regularly practising any one of the qualities above can have dramatic, life-changing benefits. You'll feel happier. You will experience greater clarity, satisfaction in life and overall life balance. Your life will take on new meaning, and you'll experience greater physical health and vitality.

Key idea

Through regular practice, we shift out of our bad habits and limiting beliefs and create lasting behaviours that support our own growth and wellbeing. It is not enough to read about these ideas, or simply to study and think about them. Spirituality is an active thing. It requires doing. The more we engage with these spiritual qualities, the more we will use them in our daily lives. The more spiritually connected we become, the closer we will find ourselves to our natural state.

These practices can also help shift your perspective from one of lack or limitation to one of abundance and optimism. These are resilient qualities that can help you move gracefully through even life's most difficult moments.

Remember this

Each day is filled with countless situations. Don't judge them as bad or good, difficult or easy. Just become aware of them. Know that everything, every situation, every circumstance, is there to serve you. This makes it easier to get through the ups and downs of the day.

WHY WE DON'T ALWAYS EMBRACE SPIRITUALITY

We know the perks that come with living a more connected life and we want to create a life that supports our self-realization, yet we fail to take consistent action towards living that life. We mistakenly believe that it's too hard, or requires too much time or energy to awaken to higher consciousness. So we fail to build in the practices required for growth.

We continue about our lives in the way we have always done. We brush our teeth, do the grocery shopping, go to work, and it's all fine. But, by the end, we realize we've lived a mundane existence prone to fear and insecurity.

The truth is that it is much harder to live without the light of spiritual energy than it is to integrate spirituality into the life you're leading.

Barriers to spiritual practice

The biggest barrier to enlightenment isn't that it's too difficult to achieve the Buddha-like state; it's that most people never try the practices to support it in the first place. We keep ourselves stuck by giving up before we even start. Here are some of the excuses we use.

▶ **Lack of time**

We hear about people who spend weekends at meditation retreats or classes, or months in solitude, and we mistakenly believe that we have to spend hours upon hours studying, practising and sitting alone to develop spiritually. 'I don't have that kind of time,' our egos shriek.

The good news is that many of the practices don't require much time; they can be fitted into our regular routine or be added simply by getting up a few minutes earlier or taking a couple of minutes during a lunch break. Spirituality is a practical way to live our life. Gratitude can be given in an instant, moving meditation can happen during a regular exercise session, and compassion is best practised during the course of your regular day. There is plenty of time for spiritual practice if you make it a priority. The best way to make sure that happens is to build it into your schedule like any other appointment, meeting or other scheduled activity.

Case study: Kate

A college professor and writer, Kate schedules time for spiritual practice into her day in the same way that she plans her classes and meets her deadlines. Every morning she meditates for 15 or 20 minutes and usually attends yoga classes twice a week. Prayer and Kirtan, ecstatic chanting, which she learned through her yoga centre, are also part of her practice. Kate studies spiritual books and attends retreats for support along her path. Church is another part of her weekly routine.

It was deep pain and despair that led her back to church. Though raised a strict Roman Catholic, Kate stopped attending mass at 19 because she found the doctrines too conservative. Instead of formal worship, she found 'spiritual solace' through yoga and meditation. It was when she was trying to cope and heal after the devastating end of a 26-year relationship that Kate began to explore her spirituality through religion again.

During her exploration, she found a welcoming and inclusive Protestant parish that elevated her spirit and offered her hope, comfort, peace and inspiration during a difficult time. It also added another dimension to her spiritual practice.

Now, despite a demanding job and other responsibilities, Kate maintains her practices and attends church on Sunday. Finding time for everything is the greatest challenge to her spiritual growth, but it's a priority, Kate says. Nourishing her spiritual dimension is 'necessary to live a complete life'.

▶ Lack of money

You don't have to buy a thing to live with greater awareness. Living in the present is free. No expensive seminars are required for enlightenment. The Internet is filled with resources for you to begin learning. Library shelves are stacked with books that can help you navigate these ideas and principles. Plenty of experts are out there offering free talks, recordings and web-based materials. As your exploration widens, you may decide to invest in regular classes, workshops or retreats, but spiritual practice requires no monetary investment. The work happens within. It's not something you buy, it's not something you wear, it isn't even what you learn – it's how you live with what you learn. And that investment starts from the inside out.

► **Lack of knowledge**

This inside-out exploration can seem daunting and difficult. People often mistakenly believe that they have to know or learn or study something before they can begin spiritual practice, but very little book learning or guidance is needed. The greatest growth and understanding occur through time devoted to practice. The rest comes from living a mindful life. Living a spiritual life is about doing, not thinking about the doing.

► **Lack of confidence**

Some of these theories can seem a little unorthodox because they require you to leave your ego behind and look at your true self. Spirituality is about tapping into energy, not necessarily something physically visible or rationally understandable. For many of us, this is a new way of being in the world, and that can feel scary. We don't know what we're going to find. Early on in the process, we don't have the faith to know that the uncertainty is a treasure to be appreciated rather than feared. It is natural to want to turn away when we don't get immediate results, or when we can't understand what we're learning.

If you can simply 'be' with these feelings, noticing your lack of confidence and fear but continuing despite them, you will realize that the feelings of confusion or uncertainty are simply growing pains. They are signs of expansion.

In reality, each of these excuses only serves to keep us stuck in the same cycle of reactivity – the place where our peace and happiness hinge on our self-image, work ethic and material success. This cycle breeds insecurity by convincing us that we are limited and broken instead of energetic souls connected to all.

Spiritual practice can hold up these and other excuses for your scrutiny. Once you see how false and empty they are, you become conscious of all that is.

Remember this

You already have all that you need to awaken. Begin today by recognizing that you are connected to the energies of this marvellous universe. Let that inspire you to begin learning more about who you already are.

Try it now

Write down five excuses that you've used to keep from trying a new spiritual practice, for example, 'I'm too tired,' 'I can't afford it,' 'I don't have time,' 'I can't sit still long enough to meditate,' 'I don't know how.'

Now, every time an excuse comes up, scrutinize it. Study it. Determine if it's true or if it's simply a way to keep you safe from the uncertainty of something new. If the excuse is keeping you trapped in the familiar unconscious, acknowledge your thoughts and step into the fear. Then try the thing you've been avoiding.

How to set up a daily practice

Daily practice is essential because it connects you to these higher energies. Through regular use of these habits and techniques, we not only experience the physical and emotional benefits but see the transforming power of awareness, faith and peace flow through every aspect of our lives.

It isn't hard to integrate these things into daily experience. Here are some ways to do it.

▶ **Start slowly.** In the beginning, as we get caught up in the excitement of our own dawning awareness, it's easy to direct all our attention to spiritual study and practice. This can lead to burnout or a stifling sense of obligation rather than expansion. Instead, pick a few practices that resonate with you and start with those, slowly adding them into your days until they feel familiar. Then expand your practice to include others.

▶ **Use time between transitions for practice.** Find a few extra minutes before or after mealtimes, or get up five minutes earlier to fit in contemplation, study or meditation. Use commuting time to pray or listen to inspirational teachings. Be mindful while taking a shower or doing housework. The more often you practise at different times of your day, the easier it becomes to live from your spiritual base.

▶ **Make each experience matter.** Spirituality isn't something that happens outside our experience; it *is* our experience.

Notice the moments of your life. Focus your attention, become present so that you become aware of your own growth.

▶ **Schedule time.** It is also useful and important to devote time each day solely for spiritual development. This should be at least 20 minutes a day (an hour is ideal). During this time sit in solitude, study, practise or meditate and simply give yourself to the moment. As with anything, the more time we spend in practice, the more skilful we become.

▶ **Quiet counts.** Each day should include moments of meditation or quiet solitude. Turn off the phone, turn down the music and simply sit in relaxed awareness. Don't judge your thoughts or try to ban them; just notice what comes.

▶ **Make time for study.** It's both inspiring and insightful to learn different spiritual practices or to read about how others are using these teachings in their own lives. Make time to read the works of others. Study the masters like Jesus and Buddha or Krishna. Pick up books that intrigue you and learn how people are thinking about and expanding the spiritual discussion.

▶ **Begin and end each day with gratitude.** Gratitude is the easiest, most powerful practice I've found to connect me to the energies of the universe. It's impossible to worry, lament, criticize or get caught up in other conditioned beliefs and behaviour when you are focused on what is going well in your life. Gratitude also breeds awareness. Challenge yourself to find new things each day to be grateful for and you'll find yourself becoming mindful throughout the day.

▶ **Have fun.** Spirituality is not a job; it's a natural state of consciousness, something instinctive, like breathing. Don't get self-righteous or serious. Don't make this hard. Certainly, don't judge yourself. This kind of exploration of the inner self is both fascinating and fun. Allow yourself to enjoy it. Play, laugh and find humour in life. Joy is a part of awakening.

Try it now

Look at this week's calendar and schedule 20 minutes each day for spiritual practice. You can break up the time and do ten minutes in the morning and ten in the afternoon if you prefer.

1 After you've set aside the time for this first day, write down how you'll spend it. Indicate whether you intend to meditate, study or practise mindfulness (discussed in later chapters). You'll find that discipline is easy to muster if you pick your practice and schedule the time the day before.

2 Then, each day after you've completed your practice time, spend a few minutes writing in your journal about the experience. What did you do? How did you feel? What were the challenges or benefits?

Focus points

✻ The best way truly to understand enlightenment is through direct experience, but the process can begin with curiosity and self-inquiry.

✻ Knowledge theory and experiential theory are two of the perspectives sometimes used when describing enlightenment. Experiential theory recognizes that you must overcome your old habits, limiting beliefs and conditions in order to awaken to your true self. Knowledge theory states that you awaken when you experience complete 'knowing' that you are consciousness and source energy.

✻ Spiritual practices are important, worth while and satisfying, whether we experience enlightenment or not. Practices including prayer, mindfulness and meditation foster wellbeing, improve physical and mental health and ease stress.

✻ People find plenty of reasons to delay their spiritual development. Most of these excuses centre on our feelings of lack. We feel that we aren't smart or worthy enough. We may worry that we don't have enough time or money to dedicate to practice and study, but spiritual practices are available to anyone at any time and can easily be integrated into our daily routine.

✻ Schedule time each day for spiritual practice and soon the practices will become habits that guide your life.

Next step

By integrating spiritual practice into our daily life we begin to awaken from the attachments and limitations created by ego. Ego isn't bad – it can be a useful tool – but when we operate only from ego it obscures our essence. In the next chapter we'll explore the role of ego and how it can help and hinder us along our path.

4

Working with ego

In this chapter you will learn:

▶ *what the ego is and how it operates*
▶ *how the ego helps and hinders our spiritual growth*
▶ *how to work with and transcend the ego*
▶ *how our spirit awakens when we quiet the voice of ego.*

Self-assessment: How does your ego show?

This quiz will give you a good idea of how ego appears and affects your actions and feelings.

1 The last time someone cut you up on the motorway, what did you do?

   a Honked and gestured at the offending driver

   b Yelled loudly in your car – but you were alone so nobody heard

   c Took a breath, decided the incident had nothing to do with you, and silently wished the driver well

2 When you forgot to pay your mortgage and incurred late charges, what did you do?

   a Blamed the mortgage company for sending the bill late

   b Got angry with yourself for being so stupid

   c Realized that everyone makes mistakes and made a note in your calendar for next time

3 How do you react when you receive recognition at work?

   a Believe the boss finally sees how good you really are

   b Decide that you just got lucky because you really have little to offer

   c Give thanks and feel mostly grateful that you can make a meaningful contribution to the planet

4 During your last argument with your partner, what happened?

   a You won, and made sure he or she knew they were wrong

   b You stopped arguing, even though you knew you were right

   c You listened closely, feeling curious rather than defensive

5 When things go differently from how you expect, what do you do?

   a Blame others and get angry about the changes

   b Blame yourself

   c Simply accept what happened without judgment or worry

6 How do you spend most of your time?

   a Doing things to get ahead

   b Doing the things you feel you 'should' do to for others

   c Listening to your intuition and then acting on faith

7 What happens when you sit down for quiet prayer, contemplation or meditation?

   a You end up making a mental to-do list of all the things you've got to get done after meditation

   b You sit quietly, but check the clock every few minutes

   c You lose track of time as you observe your thoughts

8 What do you do when you meet new people?

   a Seek out the most successful ones and try to befriend them

   b Worry about what they will think of you

   c Welcome a chance to connect with others

9 If you don't achieve your goals, how do you feel?

   a As though others have conspired against you to hold you back

   b As though you are unsuccessful and worthless

   c That the process yielded the insight and experience you needed

10 What do you believe?

   a It's up to you to make a go of it in this life

   b There is a universal source but what happens is up to you

   c If you pay attention and act with awareness, you'll see that you're part of a higher consciousness and in flow with the universe

What did you discover?

Mostly **a** answers show that you are heavily connected to your ego self. You believe you must work hard and take charge in order to prevail and that, if you don't, people and circumstances will cause you to fail. This is a tough place to live because, no matter what you do, you'll never be able to control every detail (or really any detail) required to help you ultimately feel successful.

Mostly **b** answers show that you are interested in the notion of ego and how it helps or hurts your spiritual development. You catch glimpses of how it influences your actions, but you're still unsure how to merge the ego self with your true self or spiritual essence. With awareness and spiritual practices, including many described in this book, you'll learn how the ego can help, not hurt, your exploration.

Mostly **c** answers mean that you're clear about this universal source and look for ways consciously to release the pull of ego so that you can connect more fully with the universe's higher energies.

How the ego shows

The notion of using spiritual practice to develop inner peace, mindful awareness and greater joy sounds easy enough. However, the minute we get quiet or go inside ourselves to examine our thoughts, our ego often becomes loud, clamouring for our attention in an attempt to remind us who is *really* in charge.

Part of the reason spiritual practice is so necessary and fulfilling is that it helps us to quiet those voices and manage the ego. It helps us see how our ego – an aspect of our personality – influences our lives, often by attempting to disparage our spirit. Once we recognize this, ego becomes a tool we can use rather than an unconscious nuisance that uses us.

Key idea

The ego is the aspect of our personality that creates our physical reality by balancing the basic urges and impulses of the id with the moralistic views expressed by the superego.

Try it now

Go to a mirror and spend one minute looking at yourself. Look at that face and your skin and eyelashes. Notice your nose and how the hair falls around your forehead. Continue looking and say: 'You are a beautiful, marvellous being,' and then notice the thoughts that come to mind. If it's the ego's voice, you'll hear things like, 'Don't be arrogant, you aren't that great,' or 'Whew, look at those wrinkles around your eyes.' If you don't like what you hear, redirect your thoughts to be more loving.

If you're moving in sync with your source, you'll feel a rush of love and gratitude and peace. You will look at yourself with gratitude for all your beauty and imperfections, knowing that you are part of the source.

How the ego works

Ego is the part of personality that mediates the demands of the id, the superego, and reality. The ego prevents us from acting on our basic urges (created by the id), and at the same time it balances our moral and idealistic standards (created by the superego).

While the ego operates in both the preconscious and conscious, its strong tie to the id means that it also operates at the unconscious level, making decisions for us, forming our attitudes and shaping our behaviour as though on autopilot, often without our knowledge.

Though psychologists consider the id, ego and superego as three distinct aspects of our personality, most of us experience all those dimensions coming together as a single force that we call ego. Ego is the public face of our personality. It is a visible representation of our primitive physical and social needs as well as the moral standards by which we express them. In this way, ego not only evaluates our experience of reality – based on what the ego perceives is happening to us – but it creates it.

For example, if someone cuts in front of you in line, your ego instantly juggles the desires of the id to slap the person with the needs of the superego just to behave. It then comes up with a reaction to manage the situation.

Remember this

The next time you feel like lashing out, take a deep breath and do nothing. Strong emotions are often a result of our egos mistakenly feeling threatened. If you can sit with these emotions, you'll realize that nobody is doing anything to you; there is nothing to defend.

Key idea

Psychologists believe that the ego is the aspect of our personality that creates our physical reality by interpreting our needs and desires in relation to the circumstances we encounter and then choosing a response or action. In spiritual practice, the ego is thought of as an illusion, because it fights to sustain our individuality, when in fact we are connected to all and never separate from source.

HOW THE EGO HINDERS OUR SPIRITUAL GROWTH

Left unattended, then, or unguided, the ego has tremendous power in our lives. It is often described as the core of our personality and a guiding force. The problem is that it is neither of these things. The ego is only an illusion. It is, as defined by Nouk Sanchez and Tomas Vieira in their book *Take Me To Truth*, 'a false self, the dreamer of the dream, whose voices speak to us most of the time', and it creates a state of duality, guilt, fear, chaos and suffering.

The ego creates a world with itself at the centre. It convinces us that we have to fight, strive, manipulate and control to protect ourselves. It tells us that we have to struggle individually simply to survive and that this physical existence is all there is.

When we don't work hard enough, make enough money or experience external success, we feel guilty, angry and inadequate. This is when our superego chimes in loudly with the inner voices prattling on about what we 'ought' to be doing or how we're not measuring up. This motivates the ego to do more. It gets louder and stronger and works harder to create a life that is filled with emotional and physical stuff but devoid of any lasting peace or meaning.

Left unchecked, the ego creates the illusion – that we often call reality – that we are somehow separate from source energy. It lulls us into believing that we have ultimate control and that the individual matters most and that our personal power lies in our intellect, our wealth, our status or our bodies. The more we respond to these egotistical messages, the greater the illusion becomes until we mistake it for real life and get our egos confused with our essence.

Remember this

You can quiet your ego by watching or observing the thoughts that you have. You don't have to believe or act on everything you think but, by noticing these thoughts, you begin to see when you are moving away from spirit and you can redirect.

SUCCESS AND FAILURE FROM EGO

When we buy into the illusion that each of us is an individual, separate from source, we live a physical existence that feels restless, inadequate and complicated. In an attempt to preserve our self-image, we think we always must be doing something, thriving, succeeding – even acquiring and clinging to our material possessions.

This is exhausting and leads to emotional pain because we can never do enough to satisfy the expectations of ego. Nor does this perspective provide any lasting happiness because even the successes are short-lived. You celebrate for a moment and then you get busy striving towards the next goal.

Failures are even harder to handle from the ego's perspective because they mean you are worthless. For example, you may fall into despair when someone else gets a job promotion because your ego self tells you that you failed, that you weren't good enough. It fills you with self-doubt while it pushes you to change by telling you that who you are isn't good enough.

You may get angry when someone interrupts you in a meeting, for example, because you feel that they have disrespected you. After all, if they don't listen, it means you are not valuable or appreciated, at least according to the ego's view. 'You don't deserve to be treated that way,' the ego clamours, and you are going to defend and fight and fret and stew to make sure no one else takes advantage of you.

With ego directing your thoughts and behaviour, you tend to take a defensive posture in life. You look at the world in terms of right and wrong, good and bad, and you find plenty of evidence to support your position so that you can resist and judge others. This is struggle.

Try it now

Consider a recent stressful time, a time you felt angry or threatened or disrespected. Reflect on it for a moment. What happened? Why did you feel so upset? If you felt marginalized for any reason, if you felt the need to be right or be heard, if you felt like attacking or judging someone's views or behaviour, this was a response rooted in ego. This was your ego telling you that you aren't good enough. You don't have to listen to it. Spirit never responds this way because it is never threatened.

SPIRIT IS THE GREATER ENERGY

When you operate instead from your essence, this struggle dissipates. You are no longer fighting for control. You don't need to manipulate the world for personal gain or to feel better about yourself. What you own, the roles you occupy, the car you drive, the jobs you hold, don't affect the essence of who you are. Therefore you are no longer attached to thoughts of success or failure. You are no longer clinging.

You are more focused on living with love, compassion, gratitude and contribution. The external things that do come your way, the compliments or financial abundance, then, are enjoyed instead of coveted. You are aware of them, appreciative, but no longer attached to or defined by them.

Instead, you become comfortable with the idea that you are both an infinitesimal part of the creative universe and an essential element of great magnitude.

Remember this

Next time you're tempted to express anger, take a deep breath and respond with compassion instead. This raises your spiritual energy and moves you closer to your essence and away from ego. It also just feels better.

WHAT IT LOOKS LIKE FROM SPIRIT

Now, let's say someone interrupts you again, this time while you're living from a more spiritual perspective. You're likely to notice the interruption, but you have no need to create a story around it about how you've been disrespected. You simply notice the interruption, but it has no impact on who you know yourself to be.

When you realize that it isn't all about you, but that you are a part of all that is, you step into a powerful energy stream. You are no longer operating from your unconscious, which means you are no longer led by ego. Instead, you are working with it.

THE NOISE OF THE EGO

About this time, the ego makes a last stand. This dimension of your personality is so invested in protecting you and this illusory sense of self and individualism that it's not going to go quietly. After all, the ego cannot survive without a strong attachment to the 'I'. When you merge with universal consciousness, the 'I' begins to fade and the ego begins to fight. Life can get loud.

Through the loud inner voices of self-doubt, uncertainty and fear, ego works to convince you that you are nothing without your physical body, your external self-image or your intellect. It urges you to believe that you are alone, separate from all else, and that you must fight and defend and work so that others don't hurt, harm or take advantage of you.

Without some spiritual awareness, you might actually believe these voices. Then you get scared and start planning, doing, manipulating and controlling the things in your external world to measure up to the reputation the ego expects. You push to be more successful at work. You fight to be heard, to expound your new, evolving beliefs. You may become a bit self-righteous and judgmental of those who aren't in agreement with your ideas or plans. If you need to, ego says, you can just take over and subvert the needs of others to get what you want – to become powerful.

All of this posturing serves to separate you further from your spiritual self. Your ego becomes emboldened, but you become tired, lonely and unfulfilled.

QUIETING THE VOICES

When you can let go of all of this – all these trappings that you think define you – when you can begin to quiet the ego, you begin to awaken to the knowledge that who you are is truly divine. Chaos ends, life begins to flow and the people and things to whom and which you need to articulate your purpose appear. You detach from your desires, and feel appreciation for all that appears in your life. Synchronicities happen. Opportunities emerge. Instead of paddling upstream, you are in flow with the energy of the universe.

Key idea

When you understand that you are not separate from source and it is not separate from you, the more threatened the ego becomes and the louder the voices of self-doubt, lack and inadequacy become. Just because you notice them doesn't make them true, and you can always turn your attention to your spirit.

Remember this

Source energy does not speak in disparaging ways. If you're getting an earful of insecure and insulting thoughts, that's your ego trying to take control. Recognize that and choose thoughts that feel better.

Case study: Michele

When Michele, a college professor, was chosen for an interim marketing and public relations position a few years ago, her inner voices became loud and limiting. Instead of buying into the stream of negative self-talk, Michele, with the help of a professional coach, named the voice that spouted this stream of self-defeating talk Helga. When Helga gets too loud or nasty, Michele talks back to her. It's one way to silence this belittling self-talk.

Tuning into this self-talk is just one way Michele has become more aware. She says self-awareness is the most important aspect of her spiritual life. Though she has no regular spiritual practice, Michele feels that her spirituality is woven through her days. This awareness helps her be more connected in her roles as a mother, friend and teacher and helps her stay centred and calm during times of trouble. At times – particularly when she's feeling angry and hurt – Michele also practises gratitude, focusing on at least one thing she's grateful for before falling asleep each night.

'When I'm all scrunched up and angry and closed off, thinking of the people, creature comforts and other things I am grateful for helps my heart and mind to open back up,' says Michele. Occasionally, meditation also helps her regain her footing during times of stress and quiet the voices of ego and doubt. 'It empties my brain of worries and irrelevant things and provides some peace,' she says.

Michele is committed to living a compassionate life, something she has learned more about from an unexpected source – a group of inmates in the prison writing programme she teaches. 'That's a spiritual thing for me. Some of these men have committed terrible crimes and will spend the rest of their lives in prison. But they have taught me more about grace, compassion, gratitude and forgiveness than I've learned elsewhere.'

Key idea

When you are connected to source, life flows and you no longer feel as though you have to push and strive and struggle to prove your worth. Instead, things simply appear – ideas, people, intuitions, and resources – to guide you on your spiritual journey.

THE PLACE FOR EGO IN A SPIRITUAL LIFE

As evolutionary theorist Barbara Marx Hubbard says, the ego isn't bad; in fact, it can be useful, but often it's functioning on overdrive. An over-zealous ego is divisive and keeps us from our true nature. If we can become aware, though, of how ego is working in our lives, we can regulate its impact. Then it becomes useful in helping us shape relationships, navigate the infrastructure of our physical lives, develop ideas and pursue goals with our souls directing the process.

Our higher consciousness can actually use the ego as a tool to create and grow. When we are conscious of its methods, we can prevent the ego from becoming the ultimate authority in our lives. Ego does not have to lead us. When we realize that ego is simply an aspect of our imagination, we don't have to fear it either.

Try it now

Pull out your journal and spend ten minutes describing what you would do if you weren't afraid. Ego isolates us and tries to convince us that there are certain things we have to do or be to live meaningful lives. Of course, this is all part of the illusion. Break free from that illusion by identifying who you would be, what you would do, if you weren't afraid of the ego's threats.

Transcending the ego

Our job is not, then, to rid ourselves of ego, but to transcend it: to free ourselves from the fear, to quiet those voices that conflict with our spirit, and to connect to our higher self. This can be a gradual process, one that starts with emerging awareness and ends in the complete knowing that we are whole and divine just as we are.

Key idea

Understanding how ego influences our daily experience is essential to spiritual awakening. There can be no awakening as long as we are allied with the ego's attachment to duality. Awakening comes when we recognize our unity with all.

THREE WAYS TO EASE THE GRIP OF EGO

1 Observe what you're feeling and thinking.

Don't judge, just notice. Thoughts and feelings of fear, insecurity, jealousy, worry and stress are products of our ego. Once you notice what you're experiencing, you can choose to realign with your higher self by choosing peace and love.

2 Decide not to judge.

We are in the habit of evaluating everything. As you seek to unify with source, know that judgment sits solidly in the ego's camp. When you judge, you separate yourself, find reasons to fear, and criticize yourself and others. When we are connected to source, we know that each of us has a higher purpose to fulfil. From here we can choose peace, support and love for ourselves and others. Without judgment, we have no reason to feel threatened.

3 Release outcomes and practise present-moment living.

When we function from ego, we are hyper-aware of external rewards and outcomes. For example, many people feel more successful when they receive a promotion or more money; they feel they are failures when they lose a job or their home. However, while those external events either satisfy or burden the ego, they do not disrupt our spiritual needs. If you find yourself focusing on what you're going to earn, get or buy, recognize that you are operating from ego. Instead of focusing on the outcome, become present to each moment of your life. This allows you to connect with spirit and reminds you that all you really need is love. That is the one thing that you can experience right now, because you get it by giving it away to yourself and others.

Remember this

Take five minutes each day to sit quietly and simply get to know your spiritual self. Pose questions: 'Who am I? What do I want? What feeds my spirit?' And simply listen for the answers through any physical impressions or insights. Don't judge the answers. Just begin to identify those that are emerging from your true self and those that are emerging from ego.

Hearing spirit speak

When you begin to quiet the voice of ego, when you strip away the habits of judgment and resistance, you begin to hear the voices of spirit. There is relief and a 'settling' that happens when you realize that you have all you need to exist in both the physical and spiritual planes. Ideas will seem to come in from nowhere. An energy will propel you towards purpose. It may seem as though all the people, things and information you need are simply appearing at just the right time. Pay attention to this. If you're living a spiritually directed life, this is the universe talking to you. Appreciate it. Allow it in.

Insights can be revealed in many ways, including through particular songs streaming through the radio or seemingly random coincidences that occur along your path. It happens all the time, yet we aren't always tuned in. If you're looking for guidance during this time of personal growth, look to your higher consciousness and expect messages to appear in the following ways.

▶ **Intuitive hits.** Do you ever get a gut feeling, a sense of knowing that shows up as an impression in your body or a sudden clarity? This is your sixth sense at work. It may not always seem logical or practical, but it comes from spirit and always holds something of value for you. Allow it in, and see what it has to share.

▶ **Synchronistic moments.** Famed psychiatrist Carl Jung coined the phrase to describe significant physical and psychological phenomena where two unlikely or unrelated events occur together by chance. These are the seemingly impossible or unrelated happenings that propel you towards just the thing you need or the random thing you were thinking about. Not only are these mystical moments fun, but they can also hold powerful information and encouragement. When you're paying attention, synchronicities abound.

▶ **Good-feeling emotions.** Emotions like fear, frustration and insecurity originate from ego and can give you an instant awareness that you are veering away from your true self. If, on the other hand, you are overcome by a sense of peace, of deep love, joy and gratitude, this is the universe talking to you, reminding you that you are living from a higher place. There doesn't have to be any particular reason for joy or peace to appear. These genuine emotions don't have to be prompted by a particular event, nor must they fade when difficult things happen. They are simply a part of living close to source.

▶ **Unexpected opportunities.** Higher consciousness will always move us towards what we need to connect with source. Sometimes this can feel uncomfortable. We may have to work through old habits or drop our limiting beliefs and that's alarming for the ego aspect of ourselves, which is prone to fight to prevent change. But this is also how we learn and grow on the path of enlightenment. For example, if you ask for patience, you are likely to get opportunities to practise patience. Ego won't necessarily like this, but soon you'll transcend the discomfort and recognize that all those moments that required you to sit with patience also brought you closer to spirit.

Look at the patterns in your life, the themes that seemingly appear time and time again. This is the universal source helping you to become more skilful at the things that will help you awaken.

Try it now

Think about the challenges and frustrations that have been emerging in your life over the last couple of weeks. Do they form a particular pattern? If you are having a hard time communicating with your partner, are you also having Internet issues and misunderstandings at work? Perhaps that's a sign that you should do more listening than talking. Maybe the mishaps are trying to tell you to slow down, to pay attention. Become aware of the patterns and the information they hold for you. Life holds all the experiences we need to awaken. It's simply up to us to become aware enough to use them.

Focus points

✱ Spiritual practice helps to quiet the ego.

✱ The ego is the aspect of our personality that creates our physical reality by balancing the basic urges and impulses of the id with the moral conscience views expressed by the superego.

✱ The ego is an illusion which thrives on convincing us that we are individuals who must strive, fight and work to create a life through external outcomes – money, houses, cars, friends – to be successful.

✱ When we are defensive, judgmental, fearful, inadequate and controlling, this is the ego aspect in charge. When you can give up your attachment to ego, you move into alignment with universal source and realize you are a whole, complete, unified being. This is when your life begins to flow.

✱ You can use intuition, synchronicities, awareness and emotions to gain spiritual insights and wisdom that will help you awaken.

Next step

When we cling tightly to our egos, we believe that we are separate from all else. Awakening comes when we realize this separation is an illusion. We are not alone; we are whole, source energy. Spiritual practices, like mindfulness, can help us become conscious of the illusion of ego and aware of this nodularity. In the next chapter, we'll explore the concepts of nodularity, consciousness and mindfulness.

5

Living a conscious life

In this chapter you will learn:

▸ *how some researchers explain consciousness*
▸ *levels of spiritual consciousness*
▸ *why awareness is important to spiritual growth*
▸ *the practice of mindfulness*
▸ *what* advaita *means.*

Self-assessment: How tuned in are you?

Awareness is a pivotal part of spiritual growth and it starts by paying attention. Take this true/false quiz to understand where you're starting from and to get a glimpse of where you could go.

1 You usually notice that your partner has had his/her hair cut long before he/she tells you.   T/F

2 You regularly forget where you put your keys.   T/F

3 You will be happy just as soon as you deal with this deadline at work.   T/F

4 You feel disconnected, as though you are going through the motions of life without truly engaging.   T/F

5 You tend to be more curious about your feelings than overwhelmed by them.   T/F

6 You have moments when you feel connected to all of life.   T/F

7 You are fascinated and inspired by spiritual teachings and personal development books and materials.   T/F

8 You already feel so bombarded with information that you'd rather be unconscious than mindful.   T/F

9 You are tired of the regular routine and dissatisfied with your life.   T/F

10 You find that you are able to notice and release your thoughts without clinging tightly to those ideas.   T/F

What did you discover?

If you answered 'true' to questions 2, 3, 4, 8 and 9, you're sitting in the dark and feeling the pressure. But you don't have to stay there. Peace comes with mindful awareness. This chapter will show you how to get there.

If you answered 'true' to question 9 in particular, you no longer have to feel dissatisfied, fatigued or disconnected from the moments of your life. You can tune in, become conscious of your inner landscape and the outer environment and feel your life expand with vitality, energy and insight.

What is consciousness?

The voice of ego and its incessant mental chatter can leave us believing that we are separate from all else – alone. This is an exhausting, frightening way to live. But awareness is the antidote to this isolation.

By exploring our consciousness, by becoming aware of what we are aware of, we diffuse the unconscious messages that are embedded in our old beliefs and patterns, and we become more present and spiritually connected.

So what is consciousness? Even those who study the brain have a hard time answering this question. Consciousness is a relatively new (and growing) field of study. There is no single theory on exactly how consciousness works or exactly what it is, but it is broadly defined as the relationship between the mind and the world with which it interacts.

Key idea

Consciousness is 'the perception of what passes in our own mind'.

John Locke, philosopher, 1690.

Scientists Christof Koch and Francis Crick, who worked together for a decade in the late 1990s, believed that conscious experience resides in the prefrontal cortex of our brains. Roger Penrose and Stuart Hamerhoff stipulate that human consciousness is really waves of quantum particles that collapse at certain energy levels and that neuro-pathways and cells process information in a way that produces consciousness.

Neurology professor Jacob Sage writes, 'I contend that consciousness is nothing more than the ability of our brain to acquire information (which is the state of being awake) AND all the content that the information contains AND the ability to get all that information into and out of memory.' Consciousness, he says, is a product of 'content and wakefulness'.

Still, there are plenty of people who believe that consciousness cannot be explained away as a simple reaction of neurons firing in a healthy brain. They claim that our ability to be awake and aware of our thoughts, feelings and sensations is more than a matter of brain function. Our ability to observe ourselves from ourselves is a phenomenon and a process that many believe is more intuitive than biological.

However you think about this issue, consciousness is clearly a unique ability that helps us understand and relate to our world and ourselves. The neuroscientist Antonio Damasio says that consciousness allows us to know both that we exist and that other things exist. This knowledge allows us to reach for higher levels of consciousness and greater awakening.

Levels of consciousness

Famed psychologist Sigmund Freud wrote and talked about several stages of consciousness that exist between the non-conscious – which regulates our breathing and our heartbeat and other innate bodily functions – and the consciousness experienced when we are fully awake and aware.

Try it now

Put your hand over your heart and become conscious of its rhythm. Feel the vibration of the blood pulsing out through your arteries. Feel your heartbeat. Recognize that there is much in this life that you are not conscious of, yet these things have a powerful influence over your experience. Part of becoming aware is noticing all that is occurring outside our awareness.

From a spiritual whole-life perspective, consciousness could be described as a broad continuum between unconsciousness and awakening.

UNCONSCIOUS AWARENESS

At this stage, you are operating in darkness and you don't know that there's a candle within reach. While you may look fine to others – you're physically operating in the world, working, parenting and taking care of your responsibilities – you're reactive and worried, focused mostly on surviving the day and perhaps working out ways to get more done, make more money and find more external success.

When we are unconscious, we are bound by expectation and focused on outcomes. We tend to think life is about achievement and external rewards. Our self-worth is based on how well we perform and we are at the whim of our beliefs, habits and ego.

Usually, we don't even realize the control and manipulation that our ego is exerting over our lives. We are unaware of the limiting beliefs that lie in our subconscious and how they affect our sense of self, our emotions, relationships and behaviour. In this level of consciousness, a sense of helplessness and frustration is common, and yet we think that we are functioning at our highest level.

We are truly in the dark about what is available to us and we are constantly trying to conquer obstacles so that we can get on with 'real life'.

GRADUAL REALIZATION

At this stage, you have a strong sense that what you've been doing all along is not enough any more. You are tired and unfulfilled and long for a life of greater meaning. This prompts self-inquiry and, with that, the candle of awareness ignites, lighting up the darkness a bit.

You have an intuitive sense, a growing awareness, that there is something bigger than self, something more to life than external rewards. You don't know what it is yet, but you start reading, studying and questioning. You begin practising, perhaps with some mindfulness or meditation. You're getting curious now, but you still can't seem to quiet your thoughts or get these practices right. You're still trying to work out how to apply these spiritual principles to the 'real world'. That prompts you to investigate your ego and inner voices, some of your core beliefs and your faith.

All this exploration feels a little uncomfortable and slow. The shift is happening internally, but it's not regularly reflected in your daily life. That feels frustrating at times, until you accept and surrender to whatever comes. Then the light goes on.

Remember this

You can experience instants of awakening when you allow yourself to be inspired by awesome events, transcendent performances and nature's marvels, as well as other peak moments. When we connect to the higher energy of awe, we become acutely aware of a power greater than ourselves. That motivates us to keep learning and developing our own awareness so that we can connect more often to that power in our own life.

CONNECTING TO HIGHER ENERGY

You're no longer plagued by self-doubt at this stage. You understand that the challenges are there to serve you and you know that you are part of a universal source that is guiding you. It feels as if your life is now connected to a dimmer switch that you can turn up as high as you want.

▶ You started in darkness, but your life is now illuminated by knowledge and self-awareness, love and compassion.

▶ You are no longer unconscious of the workings of the ego. You are aware of its manipulations, conscious of its limiting beliefs, and you are more responsive than reactive.

▶ You are more present in your life and your purpose is now clear. You are engaged and ready to contribute to the world in meaningful ways and you feel revitalized.

ENLIGHTENMENT

The light is fully on. The sun is out and you are not only standing in all of this white light but actually radiating it. You have experienced the awakening of self. You know God as you and you as God. There is no separation. You are no longer attached to ego; you are spirit and higher consciousness. You are the light.

Becoming aware

Spiritual development occurs, then, as we begin to turn that dimmer switch from low to high and expand our awareness from unconsciousness into the other levels of consciousness. This is the objective of many spiritual practices including meditation, chanting and mindfulness. We cannot grow spiritually or awaken to our true nature until we live with awareness in our daily lives. That is something we can learn to do.

Case study: John

'Life is a spiritual journey, whether we know it or not,' says John, a business development manager. 'The main thing to do is be aware and consciously practise that which we know will support our growth.'

For John, that practice includes meditation, walking, contemplation, simple daydreaming and witnessing, among other things. Several times a day he'll pause to focus on a feeling of love for everything as it is and also to notice and love all that is around. These practices help provide practical benefits – better health, greater joy and a broader perspective – and they help him live consciously in a non-dual state: in unity with source.

'Whatever happens, then, is a wonderful thing,' says John, 'even if outward appearances show otherwise.' Self-awareness and consciousness are intrinsic to John's spiritual experience and help him find the love within the challenge and know that things are happening just as they should, 'especially if that self-awareness is Self-awareness with a capital S,' he says. 'The more we consciously identify with our higher selves, the more we recognize the love that underlies all existence and the more we align with Divine Will.'

That insight has carried him through redundancy while buying a house, the death of his father, a new baby and a slate of daily challenges. 'In situations that look to everyone else as if my world has burned down, I'm continually as happy and at peace as I've ever been,' says John. 'Have I experienced grief and sadness? Of course, but I wasn't *in* grief and sadness, so these only added a dimension to the joy and love I have felt. When things appear to be against you, simply witness it and know it's there to create something better.'

FIVE STEPS TO GREATER AWARENESS

1 **Become aware of the present moment.** When we are looking ahead or leaning towards something else, we are often disconnected from the experience of now. We are plotting, planning and projecting what we need to get done in the next moment, the next day, the next week. We spend more time anticipating what *might* happen than engaging in what *is* happening. This keeps us in the dark. The first step to building greater awareness is to notice where you are now, in the present moment.

Remember this

If stress threatens to overwhelm you, stop, take a deep breath and become present to the sensations in your body. Connecting to our physical being is the fastest way to become present. Once we're in 'the now', it's hard to create thoughts of anxiety, fear and worry.

2 **Connect to your body.** The easiest and fastest way to become more aware is to pay attention to any physical or emotional sensations. Our body holds the clues to our unconscious and can ground us in the present moment, but when we're stressed, busy, operating from ego or focused on external symbols of self and self-worth, we often become disconnected from our physical self.

3 **Notice your thoughts.** Our minds are filled with constant chatter. We rarely recognize or pay attention to the noise, but it drones on behind the scenes, influencing our moods, beliefs and behaviour. Stop several times a day (or once an hour) and just pay attention to the thoughts coming through. Don't judge or berate yourself for having them. Just notice.

4 **Get curious.** Spiritual growth isn't about discovering any one secret and living a happy blissful life for evermore. It's about noticing the moments of the life we're already living. It's about moving consciously in the world and aligning with spirit and our very humanness. All that makes for a fascinating exploration. Get engaged in the growth. Ask questions. Challenge your existing beliefs. Scrutinize what

you've always believed to be true. Watch your behaviour. Observe the universe around you. Find new details in the familiar things. Don't judge or influence or manipulate or control. Just get curious about the universe and your place in it.

Try it now

When we become curious we engage in life and relate to ourselves in an expansive way. We inquire and question and we begin to see our thoughts with detached interest. Work with this curiosity.

Start now. Pick up something familiar that is sitting nearby – something, perhaps, that you've looked at thousands of times. Experience it anew. Challenge yourself to discover things about it that you've never noticed before.

After a few minutes of this, inquire of yourself the same way. Go inwards and ask, 'Who am I?' and discover your essence in a new way.

5 **Practise focused awareness.** Meditation, mindfulness and solitude are all helpful ways of honing our awareness and concentration. They require discipline and they begin by first noticing how restless our brains can be. We flit around from idea to idea, rarely exploring or noticing what we're experiencing in the first place.

6 **Take conscious action.** Focus on the task at hand. Give attention to what you are doing in the moment. Go patiently, trusting that, as you focus your attention, you will receive the insight and awareness you need to illuminate the next stage of your growth.

Cultivating mindfulness

Many of the steps above can be practically integrated into your daily routine through the practice of mindfulness. When we are mindful, we are paying attention in an active, open way. This allows you to detach from your experience while becoming a witness to it through observation.

This is a good thing. Not only does mindfulness alleviate stress, boost the immune system, ease pain and lower blood pressure, but it helps you feel happier, more confident and more alive. It helps you become aware of your own thoughts and present-moment experience. Once you do this, you are no longer in a reactive state, being micro-managed by your thoughts. You are aware of them.

According to mindfulness researcher Britta Holzel of Massachusetts General Hospital and Harvard Medical School, mindfulness is composed of four key components, which are:

1 attention regulation – paying attention on purpose

2 body awareness – noticing the sensations in your physical body

3 emotion regulation – identifying the emotions you are feeling (not the reasons you're feeling them)

4 self-awareness – becoming conscious of your energetic self in the moment.

When we merge each of these components in a disciplined practice of mindfulness, they help us focus our awareness on what we're feeling and experiencing in a non-judgmental way. Since worry and anxiety are products of our thoughts, a non-judgmental assessment of them can help us detach from their volatility.

Key idea

'Mindfulness means paying attention in a particular way; on purpose, in the present moment, and non-judgmentally.'

Jon Kabat-Zinn (founding director of the Stress Reduction Clinic and the Center for Mindfulness in Medicine, Health Care, and Society at the University of Massachusetts Medical School)

Try it now

Mindfully eat a piece of chocolate – spiritual practice doesn't have to be uncomfortable! Purposefully pay attention to the experience of unwrapping the bar. What does the wrapper feel like between your fingers; what does it sound like? Notice the smells. Focus only on unwrapping – don't project your thoughts on to the eating yet. Recognize the emotions and thoughts you're having. If any memories come to mind, observe and release them. Pull your attention back to the wrapper. Then feel your muscles tense to put the chocolate in your mouth. Notice the texture of it against your tongue. Continue the exercise until the chocolate is gone.

Remember this

Brushing your teeth, wiping down the worktops or driving the car can all be ways to practise mindfulness, when you purposefully bring your attention to the task.

PRACTISING MINDFULNESS MEDITATION

You don't need special equipment or an hour of time and you don't need to attend a mountain retreat or study with a monk to learn mindfulness. It can be practised anywhere, any time, and it's primarily a matter of focusing your thoughts. Here's how.

1 **Stop your activity.** Turn off the television and the music, pause for just a moment, take a deep breath and direct your attention.

2 **Start by tuning into your body and environment.** Where are you? What are you experiencing physically? Don't judge or create a story around it; just notice.

3 **Choose a focus.** As in the chocolate exercise above, choose a focus. Many people put their focus on their breath. Simply notice the repetitive pattern of air coming in and going out.

4 **Deliberately observe your racing thoughts.** When we become openly aware of the thoughts we're having, we no longer become so identified or attached to them. We become conscious of the fact that our thoughts are not us. By watching them, by getting curious about them, you step out of the judgment and the fear and the drama that often accompany your unconscious thought patterns and you transcend them. In this way, you can slowly awaken to a new level of consciousness.

CONSCIOUSNESS EMERGES FROM MINDFULNESS PRACTICE
When you integrate a regular practice of mindfulness into your life, you will find yourself becoming more conscious throughout the moments of your entire day. You become present and aware to things that you've so often passed by or failed to notice – like the traffic lights you never remember seeing on the drive to work. This infuses the day with energy and possibility. Suddenly, life feels expansive and so do you.

Remember this

If you're feeling out of sync, focus on your breath. It's a quick stress reliever and a way to expand your consciousness.

With mindfulness, our self-consciousness eases because we are not so hung up on the mind chatter and those inner voices. Mindfulness roots us in both our inner and external environments and helps to quiet the ego. It allows you to see without getting too hung up on what you're seeing. This encourages acceptance.

When you are being mindful, you are not self-criticizing, over-analysing, ruminating or worrying. You are simply being and, from that angle, life feels less threatening and more benevolent.

In this way, mindfulness fosters the expansion of consciousness because, when we are mindful to the moment, we are also aware that we are a part of it. We are no longer trapped in our heads, isolated by our individualism, but a part of the entire universe.

Key idea

Mindfulness exercises become more comfortable and familiar with regular practice. Stop for mindfulness breaks throughout your day.

Awakening *advaita*

When we have the awareness, the sense, that we are one with everything, we are experiencing what some spiritual teachers in the Hindu tradition call *advaita* or unified consciousness, the deep understanding that we are all one. That's what *advaita* means: non-dual, or not two. We are not individuals separate from our god. We contain aspects of God and we are part of a single higher consciousness.

Indian sage and spiritual leader Ramana Maharshi is known for his teachings on *advaita*. He believed that awakening to the knowing of oneness is accessible to all, through the awareness of everyday moments and self-inquiry.

'The manifold universe is, in truth, a Single Reality,' writes author and scholar Georg Feuerstein, describing the tenet of *advaita*. 'There is only one Great Being...that Great Being is utter Consciousness, and it is the very Essence, or Self (Atman) of all beings.'

'We can be unified with this higher consciousness, connected to it, without needing to appear the same,' writes Nirmala, a spiritual teacher on endless-satsang.com. There can be multiple expressions of source.

Key idea

Non-dual consciousness or awakening to the knowing of oneness, or *advaita*, is accessible to all and part of our natural state. Through mindful attention, we can experience each moment as both a part of the source and an expression of it. In this expression, it is impossible to see where source stops and our life begins. This is unity in the *advaita* tradition.

Focus points

* While there is no definitive theory on what consciousness is and how it works, it can be broadly explained as the relationship between the mind and the world with which it interacts.

* There are several levels of consciousness. As you develop spiritually, you evolve from the darkness or the unconscious stage where you are attached to the manipulations of ego and unaware of your connection to God. Gradually, you awaken to the awareness that you are one with the universal source. You become enlightened.

* You can heighten awareness by becoming conscious of the present moment, your environment and the sensations in your body.

* The practice of mindfulness promotes peace and wellbeing and enhances awareness by helping us consciously to observe our thoughts and detach from them.

* *Advaita* is the teaching that we are all one: a non-dual extension of source. Therefore we are not separate from God.

Next step

Many spiritual practices teach us to focus our attention, to become mindful, so that we expand our awareness and no longer feel our self as separate. Becoming present is a lifelong practice that can help sharpen our awareness and help us awaken. In the next chapter, we'll explore techniques for living in 'the now' and becoming more present to life.

6

Becoming present

In this chapter you will learn:

- ► *what it means to live in the now*
- ► *the benefits of being present*
- ► *how our thoughts hamper the present*
- ► *how to become more present*
- ► *how to experience flow.*

Self-assessment: Are you present?

How present are you to the moments of your life? Answer true or false to the questions here to identify your starting point. Whatever you score, remember that, with regular spiritual practice and the exercises in this book, you'll become much more comfortable living in the moment.

1 I am very in tune with what I'm feeling right now. T/F

2 I regularly use all my senses to experience my world. T/F

3 I'm a planner and like to keep a long to-do list to help me get things done. T/F

4 I often think of things I'd like to do in the future. T/F

5 When I drive to work, I'm usually thinking about what I'll need to do first when I get there. T/F

6 I usually notice small details in my environment. T/F

7 I work to take care of things right now, rather than worrying about what might happen. T/F

8 I feel stressed and uncomfortable when unexpected things come up. T/F

9 I like to be spontaneous. T/F

10 When I'm talking with people, I usually catch myself trying to figure out what I'm going to say next rather than listening closely. T/F

What did you discover?

Present-moment living isn't something we've been taught, but it is something that can be learned and practised. If you recorded mostly true answers for questions 1, 2, 6, 7 and 9, you understand the power of presence and you are working to stay present and live in the now.

Mostly false answers to those questions indicate that you are holding tight to your reality, trying to plan, predict, change and control anything that comes your way – even before it happens. This practice of attempting to manipulate the future can leave you stressed and disconnected. But you can learn to do it differently. Becoming present is simply a matter of practice, and you'll feel better for it.

Living in the moment

Living in the now. Being present. Present-moment living.

No matter how you say it, living in the moment has become the New Age rage. It's become trendy to become present. But the art and practice of paying attention have been a powerful part of spiritual practice for centuries and written and taught about by the great religious leaders and sages.

'Do not dwell in the past, do not dream of the future, concentrate the mind on the present moment,' said Buddha about 2,500 years ago. In modern times, some very good books have brought present-moment living to the forefront as a powerful spiritual practice. It immediately eases stress and helps to give clarity, insight and peace to anyone who practises it.

Living in the now means you are completely engaged in the moment – right now. You see what is here; you experience it fully. When you are present, you aren't dredging up past pain; you aren't caught up in fears of the future. All your energy is going into the moment. When you engage with life this way, you are fuelled by it.

When your focus is on past complaints or future worries, the energy that you have to deal with this moment becomes blocked and stagnant. Instead of going with the flow of what is happening, you become stuck in rumination and worry. Ultimately, any energy you have to deal with this moment dissipates.

Energy cannot be preserved by dwelling in the past; it cannot be saved up for the future. It is only by living today – in this moment – that you gain momentum to live in the next. Life takes on momentum.

Key idea

Being present is the practice of focusing and engaging solely on what is happening in the moment. There is no worry about the past or present; therefore anxiety diminishes and you feel energized and aware.

For example, when you are present, you engage and connect deeply with people, because you are not distracted or looking over their heads to see who else is coming to the party. This level of attention enhances relationships.

It helps at work, too: if you are preparing a work presentation, for instance, and you are in the present moment, focused only on the task at hand, you are better able to move through it piece by piece. In this way, you are able to pour all your creativity and resources into the presentation. This makes you more efficient. You also make fewer mistakes because you are not multi-tasking or fretting about how the presentation will be received at some point in the future. You are in the moment with a singular awareness.

 Remember this

If you are thinking about something that is over, or something that hasn't happened yet, you are missing out on the peak experience that living in the moment can provide. Use your breath to bring you back to where you are now.

When you are present, you are acutely aware that all that you have is now and you use all that you are to be a part of this moment.

 Try it now

Stop, right now, where you are, and use all your senses to experience your world. What do you hear, see, smell, taste and feel? We are most likely to become disconnected and mired in stress when we begin operating from thoughts about what 'might' happen in the future. Any time you can, stop, take a breath, and notice where you are, right now. You're bound to feel better.

The myth of past and present

Most of us have learned through a lifetime of conditioning that it's important to prepare for the future. We've learned that in order to accomplish our goals and desires, we must plan everything and take methodical, choreographed steps along the way. We hear that by looking ahead we are somehow better able to cope with whatever comes. This is a myth.

Some preparation is helpful, of course, and even possible within the context of being present. But too often we get caught up in thoughts about what has happened and worries about what is to come. This leads to a feeling of being overwhelmed.

After all, it's easy to become overwhelmed when you focus on all you have to do, instead of noticing exactly what it is you are doing. It's no wonder you feel like a failure when you're mired in thoughts of past failures instead of paying attention to the actions that you are taking right now – actions that could be successful.

To become present, we must catch our thoughts, and that is a challenge. A wandering mind is part of our biological make-up and often leads to unhappiness, say psychologists at Harvard University. When your mind wanders, according to their research, you're more likely to stew, analyse and worry. 'We reflect on our disappointments, traumas or other painful experiences – which only contributes to our unhappiness,' says Matthew Killingsworth, one of the researchers of the study.

While our ability to imagine things that aren't happening right now can be useful – as in visualization – we rarely use it in a way that is helpful. If you want to live a disconnected life filled with anxiety, then ruminating about the past and projecting the future are sure ways to do it. Studies show that distracted people experience less happiness than those who are fully engaged in a single activity.

Key idea

The human mind spends a lot of time ruminating, analysing, projecting and worrying, rather than engaging fully in the moment. This mind wandering is a source of unhappiness.

'The ability to think about what is not happening is a cognitive achievement that comes at an emotional cost.'

Journal of Science

There is only now

A mind that wanders into the past and present, but rarely resides in the now, also keeps you separate from spirit. It creates the illusion that life is fragmented, separated into categories of past and future. In time, you begin to think of these dimensions as real elements, things to manipulate or connect to – when they are not. The only way to connect with the past is from a position of right now. Mindfulness, the act of non-judgmental attention to what is, is a way to become more present.

When you are mindful, you see that life is not fragmented; it is not divided by history or time zones. Rather, it is a whole experience unified under a single source that exists and animates us right now.

Any unhappiness, then, that comes from our thoughts of separation, or our worries about the past and future, is a result of the ego getting caught up in the illusion. No wonder we feel stressed!

Remember this

Your breath is a quick way to become present. Any time you're feeling stressed, take a deep breath, focus on the air filling your lungs, and notice only that sensation. By reconnecting to the present moment, you stop worrying about the future.

THE BENEFITS OF STAYING PRESENT

When we stay present, we alleviate a great deal of the stress that threatens to overwhelm us. Much of our stress and anxiety evolves from our thoughts about what might happen in the future. Since we cannot possibly predict the future with any certainty, trying to do so leaves us feeling uncertain, stressed out and anxious.

Present-moment living is an antidote to that stress, and also a way to develop the self-knowledge that will help us cope more peacefully and gracefully with whatever comes. When we free ourselves from the drama that comes with scattered thoughts, we are more open to life and able to immerse ourselves in the moment now.

Other benefits that come with living in the now include:

- greater joy
- unencumbered clarity
- fewer mistakes
- heightened experience
- deeper social connections and relationships
- better health and wellbeing.

When we are living in the present moment, we are clear-headed and free of the distracting and ruminating thoughts that can clog up our connection to our spiritual self. These thoughts are the greatest obstacles to present awareness, but we can counteract them simply by being aware of how they appear in our lives.

PAYING ATTENTION TO YOUR THOUGHT PATTERNS

How do you stay present when you have a looming work deadline to meet and a dinner to plan the same day? How do you stay in the now if your child is home from school sick and you've a dentist's appointment to keep? How do you stay in the moment when you don't have the money in your bank account to pay the bills next week?

To become present to your life, it helps if you learn about your thought patterns so you can identify when you are *not* present. Being in the now doesn't mean you should begin to ignore all other dimensions. Of course, it's necessary to be mindful of those future work meetings, activities and commitments. But awareness can only happen in the present.

BRINGING YOUR THOUGHTS TO THE PRESENT

Being present is about managing your thoughts when they come up *now* instead of letting them run away with you. When we are living unaware, one thought leads to another and another and soon we've created an entire illusion based on what *might* happen, instead of what *is* happening.

When you catch yourself obsessing over what might have been or what is to be, stop the cycle by changing your physiology. Stand up or sit up straight with both your feet flat on the floor and get physically grounded. Notice the feelings in your body as it becomes centred in its environment right now.

Of course, we often revert to thoughts of the past or future. You may spend the entire day becoming aware of your projections and ruminations and returning to the present moment. That's okay, as long as you become centred in the present again. It is the only thing that is real.

Try it now

Think about a short chore or responsibility that you must complete before the end of the day. Write it down. Do not describe it; just state what it is.

Now, take a deep breath and get centred in your body, and become aware of your feelings right now.

Then begin working on the task. Observe your thoughts as you go. Keep them focused only on an aspect of the chore you must do right now. Once this aspect is completed, go on to the next. Take one step at a time. Don't multitask. Just focus your thoughts until the job is done.

PRODUCTIVITY RESIDES IN THE PRESENT

We are often much more productive and efficient when we focus our thoughts on what we are doing right now. When we fall into the trap of remembering the past or considering future outcomes – such as how our project will be received or how well we did or didn't do it last time – we become less creative and more stressed. We lose valuable work time. Multitasking also leads to error.

Key idea

It's common for our thoughts to wander, but this is neither a peaceful nor a happy condition. Set the intention to become present and notice your thoughts. This will help you bring them back to the present moment when they stray. Do this and you'll be happier and more productive.

HOW WE GET DERAILED

We don't intend to lose track of the moment. In fact, we often don't even know it's happened. Even so, Harvard researchers say our minds wander nearly 50 per cent of the time.

It happens like this. Say you decide to cook fish for dinner. As you begin seasoning the cod, you flash on a memory of the last time you cooked fish for your parents. The dinner erupted in anger when your father didn't like the recipe and you felt insecure and unappreciated. Now, preparing dinner in an entirely different kitchen, months or even years later, you get stuck back there in those bad feelings from the past. You are no longer present.

The next time this happens – and it will – don't be angry with yourself. Simply become aware of the disconnection, and then move into the moment by centring your body and observing your thoughts. After that, reset your intention to remain present and start again. Experience the peace that comes when you realize you caught your thoughts before they derailed you entirely. There is power in this. The more often you do it – catch your wandering mind and refocus your attention – the easier it becomes. Ultimately, your powers of attention and concentration will grow.

Case study: Ron

For Ron, a creative director, focusing the mind is an essential part of his spiritual growth and his spiritual exploration.

'It's really a process of closing off my mind to external influences', he says. Sometimes he does this by focusing his awareness on his breath before falling asleep; at other times his focus stays on a big question during a 15-minute contemplation practice.

Self-awareness, he says, is at the core of his spiritual practice and the method that generates spiritual and personal growth. His practice is fluid and organic, often shifting and changing depending on his work schedule and the needs of his wife and two daughters. Ron finds pockets of time for spiritual practice in the middle of his day. Sometimes that is during mass with his family or while travelling on the bus, or driving alone or even while in the bathroom.

'Skiing and hiking, when I get the chance, are profound spiritual experiences for me,' he says. 'My church of choice is on the saddle of a bicycle – riding is also a critical part of my spiritual practice.'

Over the years, his spiritual practice has been varied and diverse. He has studied Buddhism, existentialism, psychology and Freudian psychoanalytical theory as well as Greek philosophy. He has repeatedly read Hermann Hesse's novel *Siddhartha*, practised Ayurveda and yoga, and contemplated the connection between the laws of physics and the existence of spiritual beings. He has built voodoo shrines and bantered with Hare Krishna followers, and he says that spiritual exploration helps him find his way back to a better understanding of himself.

'I can be a pathological extrovert, letting the external world thrash me about, letting others determine the course of my actions, and even, at times, my thoughts,' says Ron. 'Yoga eases physical pain and stress, but it also helps me access that inner self more easily. My spiritual life is like gravity, a force pulling me towards my core, my true self. I just have to stop being a rocket and pulling away from it.'

It is possible to stay present *and* deal effectively and easily with the commitments, responsibilities and goals in your life. To do so requires mindfulness and focus but, in return, you will live an inspired and engaged life – right now.

Signs that you are not living in the present include the following.

► You feel as though you need relief from the busyness of your life, so you drink, shop, surf the Internet or take on other mindless distractions to relax.

► You feel as though you are always in a hurry.

► You make mistakes, probably as a result of multitasking.

► You're forgetful.

► You experience niggling colds and illnesses.

► You feel disappointed about missing out on things that might have been fun or helpful.

► You feel disappointed because events you anticipated didn't live up to your expectations.

How to live now

When you live in the present moment, you awaken to it; you become aware of the energy and the connection and the unity that connects each of us, everywhere, to this single moment. This awakens a subtle shift in consciousness that changes how you view everything. From that shift comes peace and tolerance and compassion – the language of spirit.

Here are seven ways to be more present to your life.

1 **Observe rather than react.** Reaction often requires analysis or some ego-based assessment or judgment of what happened. Observation does not. You don't have to react; you can simply notice and experience whatever is going on through your five senses. Your observations may lead to action, but when you are fully present, your choices are clearer and often you realize that no response is required. It's when you start seeing things through the filters of the past and future that you feel threatened, defensive or trapped, and become utterly reactive.

2 **Schedule present-living moments.** It's hard to be developing a habit of mindful presence when you're rushing around all the time and forgetting to practise. Plan times throughout the day for a small, in-the-moment break. Pick at least three times each day to stop and be still for five minutes and simply notice what is within and without. Don't judge; just notice.

3 **Create speed bumps around daily rituals or chores.** Find pockets in the middle of your daily schedule to slow down and become present. Living an awakened life means that you are aware of the life you are living. Create space for this awareness to flourish by adding mindfulness to your daily routine. Decide to do various activities, such as brushing your teeth or eating your meals, mindfully. When you are in conversation, vow to be fully engaged. Do not worry about what you're going to say or how to react; simply be there and pay attention to all that emerges. Before you go for a drive, pay attention to the present moment of touching

the steering wheel and the feel of the seat along your back. Commit to driving with the radio off and becoming present at each traffic light.

4 **Notice what you're feeling.** If you feel overwhelmed or stressed, catch your thoughts in that moment and look at their origin. Are they about future challenges or past hurts? If so, bring them back to just now. Root them in the sensations of your body and the immediate details of your environment.

5 **Widen the view.** As you begin to develop your present-moment awareness, allow it to expand. Start by becoming present to the sensations of your body. Then expand your view to your immediate environment. What does it look and sound and smell like? Then move further out to the present-moment sounds you can hear, such as the wind blowing against the house or the sunlight reflected on the window. Then go out a little wider, to the sky and the clouds, and perhaps the moon showing through the blue sky in this moment, and then to the galaxy that envelops us and the universal mind. From present-moment awareness grows our connection to higher consciousness. That is powerful.

6 **Take one thing at a time.** Becoming present requires no doing at all. You don't have to change or improve or fix. You simply have to be with what is, noticing it. When we multitask, we are not only prone to error, but we become disconnected from our inner self and our inner knowing. This leads to projections about future failures and past memories of inadequacy. Stop it. Do one job and focus on each step along the way. When it's complete, do the next. Fully engage in each part of the process, no matter how small.

7 **Be free and open with what comes.** When you step in with thoughts of judgment or intolerance, you are stepping out of present awareness. Focus only on what presents itself. Do not get stuck in your opinions, evaluations or judgments. Stay present to whatever is happening instead of thinking about what you would like to happen.

Try it now

Sit down, close your eyes, and imagine yourself in the middle of a giant circle. Now, move into present-moment awareness. What is next to you in the circle? What can you touch or experience directly? What is just beyond your reach in that circle? Can you take a broader view now? Expand your perspective further. Imagine your circle stretching out across the street, extending into the nearby environment and out into space. Become aware of all that is part of your expanded view right now. What do you notice? Your life is not defined by limiting thoughts borne from where you've been and where you're going. Your life is now.

Flow and present-moment living

It is only when we are fully engaged in the present moment that we can delve deeply into our passions, explore our purpose, and step into the flow of the universe. Flow, as defined by pioneering psychologist Mihaly Csikszentmihalyi, is the state of total absorption. You become so engaged in your experience in that moment that you lose the sense of everything around you. Time falls away; limits are non-existent.

This state is more likely to occur when you're doing something that is challenging but achievable. In fact, you expect challenges to appear, but you are so present that you just take care of things as they arise, with little thought or worry about the future.

Imagine what would have happened if the one of the greatest basketball players of all time, Michael Jordan, worried about whether he would make his next shot, even before he shot the first. Instead, he focused and immersed himself in the flow of the game. He became aware of what was required to make his first shot. Then he moved on to the next. He took it one step at a time. Of course, Jordan knew there were other shots and other games, but he took things as they came, taking the shots as he had them, in tune with the game he was playing at that moment.

When you're in flow, you are aware of some of what is to come, but you're not attached to it. You don't worry, dwell or focus on the future. You participate in the moment that is present.

WHEN DOES FLOW OCCUR?

Flow cannot be cultivated, contrived, or created. It comes when you are engaging in life, when you are paying attention and participating fully in the moment. Many people report feeling in flow when they are engaged in their life's purpose, or creating art, playing sports, climbing mountains or dancing and playing music. The best way to experience flow is to experience life and pay attention to what happens.

Remember this

You don't have to beat yourself up for not staying present to every moment of your life, but use mini-moment breaks throughout your day to ground yourself. To do this, stop what you are doing, take a deep breath, and notice everything that is part of this particular moment. If you take five mini-moment breaks throughout the day, you will remain more connected to now.

Focus points

✻ Living in the now means you are completely engaged in life – right now. In present-moment living, you are mindful of what is going on around you and within you. You aren't dredging up past pain; you aren't caught up in fears of the future. You are engaged in the now.

✻ Feelings of anxiety or stress are a result of focusing your thoughts on the past or future rather than the present.

✻ People who live with mindful attention on the present experience greater joy, less stress, fewer errors, greater productivity, better health and deeper connection to the divine.

✻ You can develop a practice of living a more present life by slowing down, doing one thing at a time, focusing on your breath and the sensations of your body, and being open to outcomes without judgment.

✻ Flow, that exhilarating state of total absorption, can be a product of present-moment living.

Next step

Becoming present and mindful is an exhilarating and less stressful way to live. In order for us to awaken into the realm of higher consciousness, not only must we become present but we must also become free from resistance and judgment. The next chapter will explain acceptance and resistance and describe how we can use adversity *en route* to self-actualization.

7

Ending resistance, embracing acceptance

In this chapter you will learn:

- ► *what resistance is and why it hurts*
- ► *what acceptance is and how it heals*
- ► *how we can make a conscious choice to embrace acceptance*
- ► *that acceptance leads to self-awareness and lets us see the world more clearly and honestly*
- ► *how to thrive during challenging times.*

Self-assessment: Are you a fighter?

Take this quiz to find out how resistance shows up in your life and then we'll discuss how to move through it.

1 What do you like doing after a hard day at work?

   a Have a couple of glasses of wine and watch mindless television

   b Gossip about the crazy things your boss does

   c Consider what you're feeling and recognize that difficult emotions are sometimes a part of life

2 The last time you faced a major challenge, what did you do?

   a Kept busy so you didn't have to deal with the stress

   b Felt as though life was unfair and the difficulties shouldn't be happening to you

   c Acknowledged what was happening and also gave thanks for the other positive things in your life

3 What do you do when you go after a goal?

   a Believe that battling through obstacles is the only way to accomplish what you desire

   b Try to avoid others who you think may hinder your success

   c Pay attention to what you're learning along the way and adapt when obstacles surface

4 What was the reason for the last argument you had with a friend or partner?

   a They didn't do what you expected

   b They made a mistake and you decided to set them straight

   c You reacted in anger instead of recognizing the fear you were feeling

5 What do you think when things are going well in your life?

   a Worry that it's just a matter of time before things turn sour again

   b Wonder how you got so lucky

   c Take time to enjoy the good feelings and give thanks

6 How did you react during one of the bad times in your life?

   a Felt angry with God

   b Told everyone who would listen about your woes and fears

   c Worked to stay in the present to live each moment consciously

7 When the unexpected comes up, what do you do?

   a Work hard to get through it, so things can return to normal

   b Get angry and stressed. Can't you have a moment of peace for once?

   c Get curious and look at every side of the situation

8 How do you react when someone gives you a compliment?

   a Deflect it by changing the subject

   b Say thank you, but feel like a fraud

   c Say thank you, and let the words sink in

9 When confronted about a weakness, what do you do?

   a Deny it and believe the other person is wrong or out of place

   b Feel embarrassed to be 'found out' and promise to hide it better next time

   c Become curious, step back and take a truthful look at the situation.

10 When do you usually feeling stressed?

    a When things didn't go as planned

    b When you're worried about the future

    c When you haven't slowed down long enough to experience the present

What did you discover?

Again, there are no wrong answers here. If you're like most of us, you have probably experienced all the choices listed for each question at one time or another. However, if you caught yourself circling predominantly **a** and **b** answers, you're making this life experience harder than it has to be by fighting against what is. This can cause you to feel uptight, stressed, stuck and unhappy. Acceptance is an easier way.

Awakening

As we continue along this path to awareness and awakening, we become more and more conscious of the lives we're leading. We are getting clear, becoming honest with ourselves, and noticing the places that are full and vital and love-filled and the holes that seem to separate us from our essence.

We are in the process of knowing 'with a capital K', as healer and spiritual teacher Paul Hertel describes this process of spiritual opening. More and more we'll experience moments of awakening as we shift into our higher consciousness and unify with the universal source.

What happens when what we are awakening to doesn't feel good? What do we do when the present is pain-filled? What happens when the life that we are leading feels frightening, painful and hard? We can even learn to accept all that and find some measure of peace.

The practice of acceptance becomes vital as we grow into our spiritual selves. It not only eases pain but helps us to become clear about the realities of our lives. It guides us through the illusions and resistance that so often hold up our growth and contribution. Part of learning to accept your experience as it is is also to acknowledge the places where you might be resisting your reality.

How resistance appears

Resistance rises up when we blame, excuse, label, assume or create expectation or denial around a situation or circumstance, outcome or emotion. When we push against what is really happening by judging or telling a story around it, we are resisting. When we start wishing that things were different, or lamenting that something shouldn't have happened, we are resisting and sabotaging our own growth.

Anything that moves us away from the truth of what really is causes resistance and assures us of one thing – that we'll be stuck in a painful place. You cannot accept what is, or even see it clearly, until you give up your resistance. The way out of resistance is to recognize that you're fighting against the truth in the first place.

Key idea

Resistance is at the root of our pain. Whenever we excuse, deny, blame or otherwise fail to see what is already happening – what already is – we are in resistance. Until we take an honest, non-judgmental look at the realities, we'll remain stuck and in pain.

Below are two examples of how resistance shapes our reactions and limits our lives by obscuring the truth.

EXAMPLE 1: RESISTANCE IN THE WORKPLACE
Situation: Your boss suggests that you need to improve your communication skills if you'd like to move into management.

Root of resistance: This makes you feel a little uncertain and insecure. You feel hurt. Instead of acknowledging these emotions, you resist them.

Reaction: You gossip about the boss to co-workers. You blame him for being hypercritical and not liking you. You begin to attack his own abilities – after all, he's not a great communicator, either. You make excuses; perhaps you grew up in a family that never talked, so how are you supposed to be any better? It's not your fault. Then, to add to your stress, you create a story about how you are unappreciated and disrespected.

Instead of considering his comment for what it is, your ego takes offence and you combat the bad feelings by embellishing and dramatizing the situation rather than looking at the validity of his statement. You resist improvement and never get the recommended training; therefore your chances of promotion are doomed.

Truth of acceptance: If you cultivate your ability to see life honestly, you are not threatened by comments from your boss or anyone else. You quiet the ego and allow your spiritual self to emerge into a place of truth. This gives you an accurate view of the situation and that clarity helps you to choose an appropriate action.

Sometimes the action is to do nothing, but it could also allow you to go confidently forward to upgrade your skills, which puts you in line for that promotion. If you stay stuck in resistance, you will fail to move forward and get the training required. The job passes to someone else.

With acceptance, the angst stops and opportunities emerge. With resistance, pain prevails.

EXAMPLE 2: RESISTANCE IN RELATIONSHIPS
Situation: Your marriage is no longer satisfying or loving.

Roots of resistance: You feel afraid and uncertain when you recognize that you are unhappy in your marriage, so you decide not to deal with it. You avoid talking about anything important with your partner. Things only get worse. As time goes on, you leverage blame, numb yourself to the experience through alcohol, work or other relationships, and eventually you find yourself making more and more excuses for what isn't working.

'We're just so busy,' you say. 'We'll reconnect when things slow down.'

Reaction: Slowly, the joy leaves your household. Because you are denying the problems in the relationship, you are not working to fix or learn from them either. The pain of resistance engulfs you. You feel exhausted and resentful. You seek relief, however temporary, in unhealthy ways. You begin to drink more. One of you has an affair. Now, aside from all the difficulties of the relationship, you have that to deal with.

Truth of acceptance: With acceptance, you could see the truth – that you work too much and haven't taken time to nurture your relationship. You would notice that you no longer feel connected, and that both of you are unhappy. From that position of knowledge, you have something to work with, a starting point. You can begin to work with your spouse to improve circumstances, sign up for counselling, cut back your hours at work or end the relationship. There is nobody to blame. It's all just information you can use.

When you stay in resistance, you are closed to that information and stuck in the same depleting story, the same unhappy situation, day in and day out.

STOP TELLING THE STORY

The story clouds the truth, limits our awareness and often prompts us to become reactive. Then we take actions on a set of criteria that are part of the story we have created but are rarely part of the actual circumstance. The actions and emotions we feel at this point usually move us further from the truth of our experience until we're unhappy and standing in the dark.

Stop telling the story. Just become present to what is, describe it without judgment. From this position of truth, you'll know what you need to do to align with your higher self, a self that is open and expansive and free from the pain of resistance.

The pain of staying stuck

Resistance – denying what is – only results in pain and limitation. When you move into denial, anger, wishing or controlling, you get stuck in the judgments or expectations surrounding a situation, instead of dealing with what is actually happening.

This is like swimming in the ocean. Imagine that you are out there, floating among the waves, when you see a giant wall of water coming towards you. If you deny its power, resist the danger, make excuses (I didn't know it was going to be rough out here today), you'll leap right into the crashing wave and it will knock you back, bruise your body and push you away from the calmer waters. But, if you see that wave, and you accept its powerful nature, you know what to do to work with it. You know how to move with it. You stay low near the surface, or dive just below it and become a part of the current, riding with the wave.

Remember this

Just because something feels unfamiliar doesn't mean you're heading the wrong way. A shift to higher consciousness and an awakened state is going to feel different from what you know. Don't turn away during these moments of expansion. Be curious and lean into them. Notice the discomfort, but don't turn it into something negative.

Try it now

Take a deep breath. Feel the air going in through your nose, feel it cool against your throat. Notice your belly expanding. Now exhale and again notice the air as it goes through. It's refreshing, enlivening and animating. Now, with your index finger and thumb, pinch your nose closed and take in another breath, again through your nose. Don't open your mouth. It's hard to do, isn't it? You have to fight for that bit of air. Now, again, exhale through your nose. You have to push and strain to do something that is usually very instinctive, easy and natural. That is resistance – and it feels hard and painful wherever it occurs in your life.

Key idea

Much of our resistance and denial come from the story we create around any given situation. Relief comes when we stop dramatizing the events of our lives. Notice them, become aware of the nuances, and experience all of that without judgment.

Acceptance: the conscious choice

Living a spiritual life is also about living a conscious one, and acceptance is a key to consciousness. The good news is that you can begin the habit of acceptance right now. You can feel better, now. But, you've got to break some bad habits. We are experts at judging, blaming, excusing and denying our reality; we are used to fighting against what is in order to get what we think we want.

We've become comfortable with the idea that life is hard, that you've got to push, work and strive to get ahead. Life is not that hard, though, when you're working from spirit. Your essential self is energy and light. That means that, when you align with your true nature, you also align with the elements that make up the vast universe. It's all perfect as it is and you are a part of it all.

You don't need it to be any different. You no longer have to fear the truth, or alter the perception. You can simply observe what it is, knowing that it does not define you and cannot hurt you – unless you create the story around it. When you reach this place of knowing, you are free of the shackles of resistance and able to live from the powerful place of acceptance.

Remember this

In martial arts training, students are taught to yield to the force and move with the opponent's energy, instead of trying to push back. This leaves your opponent off balance, thus giving you the upper hand. Next time you catch yourself making an excuse, blaming others or denying something, yield to the truth of it and step into the flow.

Try it now

Pull out your journal and for two minutes write about a situation that has upset and bothered you. Write quickly.

Now take a look at what you wrote and describe the problem in one sentence, no longer than ten words. Boil it down. Say only the truth. Once you can see the reality, unclouded by judgment and opinion and angst, you can accept it. Then you have something to work with.

THE TENSION OF RESISTANCE, THE EASE OF ACCEPTANCE

When we are in resistance, we embellish the truth. But, living with delusion only keeps you caught up in it. With acceptance we see clearly.

Notice the way the energy shifts between the two perspectives. One feels constrictive and narrow, the other expansive.

▶ Resistance: I can't believe this is happening, I'll never be successful.

▶ Acceptance: I didn't get the job, and I'll need to find another way to pay my bills.

▶ Resistance: I wish I were healthier, but I just don't have time to cook healthy foods.

▶ Acceptance: I am 20 pounds heavier than I'd like.

▶ Resistance: Of course I'd like to improve my skills, but my boss won't pay for the training so there is nothing I can do.

▶ Acceptance: Right now, I don't feel confident enough to get more training.

When things feel difficult, it's usually because we are resisting what is taking place. Once you identify the areas you're resisting (and we all have them), once you see what you're denying, you awaken with a new clarity and a relief so profound that you'll feel physically lighter.

Try it now

Take a closer look at three situations in your own life that aren't working as planned. What is the truth about these situations? What is the reality?

Write down your responses so you can see the truth clearly, unadorned. Now, over the next couple of days, come back to these areas of your life and write in your journal about any new insights you receive about them. When we get clear about our life, we also get clear ideas about how to cope with it.

ACCEPTANCE IS NOT QUITTING

Acceptance doesn't mean that you give up, or quit, or put up with bad or difficult situations. It doesn't mean that you think everything is all right the way it is, or even that you're happy with how things are. It is simply a way of seeing what is, so that you can choose the appropriate responses or actions that will move you closer to your spiritual self and into the freedom that comes from that.

Acceptance also makes way for self-compassion and compassion for others. It opens up avenues to love, curiosity and connection. When you stop fighting and pushing, you have more energy to focus on the now and you begin to move through the things you so long denied. This moves you into flow and expansion.

FOUR STEPS IN THE PRACTICE OF ACCEPTANCE

1 **Evaluate what isn't working.** Look at the excuses you make and the blame you levy. Check out the areas where you haven't made the progress you desire. Are you still trying to lose that last 20 pounds? What are you wishing and hoping for instead of making it happen? These are indications that resistance is at work.

2 **Delete the story and judgment.** Now take a look at the area you've identified and eliminate the story around it. Cut the judgment; there's nothing wrong. There's no need to beat yourself up; just acknowledge that, for the first time, you are seeing the truth and simply declare what it is.

3 **Notice mind chatter.** Once you become clear, you'll experience some fear, perhaps even some self-doubt and the inner voices of ego will push you back towards judgment. Acknowledge these voices, hear them and let them pass. You don't have to give them any attention, nor do you need to shut them up. Just allow them to float through.

4 **Focus energy on what is.** Now that you are clear, you can deal with this dawning reality in a more proactive way. You are no longer stuck in the same old destructive or stifling patterns. You are open instead of resistant.

Instead of saying, for example, that you 'just like to have a couple of glasses of wine to unwind after work', by taking the four steps you will become aware that you are drinking too much because your job is unsatisfying. With that information, new choices are available to you. You can get help for the wine habit if needed, find healthier releases, get a new job, find a way to make the job you have more interesting, rediscover other passions, or decide to do nothing at all.

Until you get clear through acceptance, you can't see the challenges before you and you can't identify the solutions. You are living in a state of darkness or unconsciousness. The truth of acceptance leads to greater self-awareness, which will guide you towards awakening and a life that is much more peaceful.

Key idea

When you gain clarity through acceptance, you can effectively respond and engage in any aspect of life because you are dealing with honest, true information. When you see what life is – without the resistance – each circumstance and situation becomes clear and so do the solutions and possibilities.

GOING WITH THE FLOW OF WHAT IS

Acceptance is peace and flow. It allows you to be present and live life as it is. Because you are no longer afraid of the truth, you are capable of living with it and free to dedicate all of your abilities, love and talents to any given situation. You are able, then, to engage in life, to live it fully as it is, and to awaken to all that is.

Remember this

Acceptance is a choice. Each day, each moment, you can choose to remain mired in resistance and spend your time working and manipulating rather than seeing what is actually before you. Alternatively, you can choose to accept what is and work with it. Try choosing acceptance next time you're stressed about a situation and see how fast the bad feeling moves into something better.

Case study: Jennifer

It was while coping with grief over her father's death that Jennifer got an unexpected lesson in acceptance. His passing left her with many unanswered questions and, as she went deep within herself to find solace and understanding, she also gained great clarity.

'Ultimately, the inner examination led me to acceptance – acceptance that I may never understand some things, and the knowledge that I can't change what happens.'

This realization helped Jennifer, a clinical research associate, move through her confusion, anger and sadness. And, it's through this kind of self-examination that Jennifer continues to practise acceptance in her life. With acceptance, she's able to deal with challenges instead of denying them.

Though she considers herself a 'semi-practising Catholic', Jennifer says she doesn't feel the need to go to church to feel closer to God. She can connect to her spiritual side while walking beside a lake or in the woods, and even while walking on the treadmill. By fostering this conscious connection to spirit, she says she's able to find the peace and clarity that helps her accept life circumstances.

'There's no right or wrong way to find or develop your spirituality, but I do believe that introspection and self-awareness are key,' says Jennifer. 'Don't be afraid to be alone with your thoughts or even to be alone with your person for a day or two. I think it's important to shut the world out on occasion and really to listen to your inner being. When I do that, I seem to gain greater appreciation for the people in my life as well as a renewed perspective on my own life.'

How acceptance can help during challenging times

Acceptance does not conquer pain – though it helps – nor does it mean you'll never face a challenging time. Many of our challenges are a result of the incongruities that arise between who we know ourselves to be – energy unified with the universal source – and the experience we're having as parents and partners and people trying to make it in this physical world.

Remember this

You don't need to silence the inner voices to reach acceptance; you need simply to acknowledge them and let them move freely through your mind. Don't attach yourself to them or cling to them, or even believe them. Notice them and let them go.

Acceptance can ease these incongruities. You cannot be divided when you side with the truth. When you are clear, you become more aware and conscious. Then, when the challenges come up, you experience them differently; you are no longer overwhelmed by them. You no longer attach yourself to outcomes in the same way and your self-worth no longer depends on what others think, because you know the truth of who you are.

In this way, acceptance is a practical choice for those who want to live more spiritually based lives. It takes off the bindings and allows room for spiritual and personal expansion. It's also a good way to deal with the difficult moments that crop up unexpectedly.

Next time your thoughts are running away from you and you feel you're fighting life rather than flowing, try these tips to get clear, accept the situation and ease the anxiety.

► **Restate:** There are multiple ways to look at any given situation. When we are scared or caught up in resistance, we're usually creating some false drama around the actual circumstance we're facing. Next time you catch yourself ruminating, stop and challenge yourself to come up with another angle – one that will move you closer to the truth. For example, 'I didn't get the call back for a second job interview. I knew I was horrible and had no chance of being hired,' can be more accurately restated as, 'I didn't get a second interview.'

► **Get real:** Become present and then look at what you are sure you know, right now. Resistance gains a foothold when we're projecting or dwelling. Root yourself in the moment. Notice your lungs expand as you breathe. See the wrinkles in the skin around your knuckles. Consider the challenge you're facing in terms of only what is true at this moment.

▶ **Give thanks:** Gratitude is a quick link to spirituality and a way to shift out of distress almost instantly. Good remains even when troubles surface. Move your energy from the resistance of what is into acceptance of all that is well. Acceptance isn't only useful when things are going badly, but it's a powerful and authentic way to experience all of life. See the things that *are* working in your life: you are breathing, you have eyes to read this book, you are a creative human being. Give thanks for these things and feel resistance shift to openness.

Try it now

Shift from resistance to acceptance in the moment by making peace with your inner thoughts.

Take a deep breath, close your eyes and consider a problem or frustration you're facing right now. Notice the stress and tension it creates in your body. Feel the tightness and think about the issue that is stressing you. Look at it clearly and quickly. See the truth of it. Then, shift your focus to all the open space around that place of tension in your body. Watch that open space expand until the openness absorbs the tension. Watch it dissipate.

Focus points

* Resistance is when we deny, blame, dramatize or otherwise obscure our view of reality.
* Resistance leads to stress, anxiety and unproductive actions. When you are unaware of what the truth of a situation really is, you cannot respond to it proactively.
* Acceptance is when you clearly see and acknowledge the truth of a situation without judgment, opinion, blame or dramatization.
* Acceptance is relief, peace and inspired action. When you know what you're facing, you can respond appropriately and powerfully.
* You can choose acceptance in the moment, by recognizing your connection with source and choosing to trust that all happens just as it should.

Next step

Resistance keeps us in a cycle of denial, drama and anxiety. Acceptance frees us to experience all that is, as it is. Then we gain a clarity that lets us move forward, to change our circumstances or surrender to what is. Letting go or surrendering is a powerful spiritual practice that we will explore in depth in the next chapter.

8

Learning to surrender

In this chapter you will learn:

- ► *what surrender is*
- ► *how to cultivate the active process of surrender through practice and attention*
- ► *how to give up control and experience greater peace*
- ► *how surrender springs from faith*
- ► *how to connect to your faith.*

Self-assessment: Are you holding too tight?

How good are you at giving up and giving in, letting go and letting God operate in your life? Take this true/false quiz to identify what you know about surrender and to learn what you can do to help ease the stress and angst that come when you are holding too tight.

1. Every time something does not turn out as planned, I step in and try to fix it.   T/F

2. I tend to do the best I can and just roll with whatever happens.   T/F

3. I believe that there are larger forces at work than what I can see and touch.   T/F

4. If I 'give up' or let go, nothing will get done.   T/F

5. The concept of surrender implies quitting and I am not a quitter.   T/F

6. When I stop trying to manage things, it seems that the things I need the most appear in my life.   T/F

7. I feel deep sorrow and sadness about some of the bigger mistakes I've made.   T/F

8. If things don't go the way I'd like, I get very upset.   T/F

9. I feel so much better when I'm not nagging and controlling.   T/F

10. I often have to remind myself just to let go.   T/F

What did you discover?

'True' answers to questions 2, 3, 6, 9 and 10 indicate that you have already experienced some of the benefits of surrender by allowing things to unfold and develop. If your answers show the other side, though, the one that likes to control and manage things to make them happen, you're experiencing the pain of resistance. You'll find great relief in learning to surrender to it. Sometimes it's all we can do.

Surrender: an active way out of pain

One of the greatest obstacles we encounter along our spiritual path is the ego's desire for certainty. We believe that, if we work hard enough, if we do the right thing, we can control what happens in our lives. Our attachment to the idea that we are the ones with ultimate control is one of the things that adds to our suffering when things go awry.

You know those moments. You plan for a single goal, a particular outcome, the happy ending, and then find it hard to function or even survive when things don't go according to plan.

▶ Perhaps you've waited 20 years for the CEO position, only to watch it handed to someone else.

▶ Maybe you've been a healthy eater who regularly exercises, only to learn that you have cancer.

▶ You've prided yourself on a strong, enduring marriage, only to find out that your partner has cheated.

When things fall apart, often we do too. This happens primarily because we've been holding on so tightly. We've created so many expectations and become so attached to the people and places and things in our lives that we are devastated when those things change or disappear. But change is the nature of life and learning to surrender to the flow of life is a pivotal way to awaken spiritually and ease suffering. The only way to peace is to surrender our control.

Remember this

Next time you're feeling unhappy about a particular outcome, let it go, just for a while. Set aside time – maybe ten minutes, an hour or a day – when you will detach from it completely. Don't do anything about it. When we can release our troubles, even for a while, we see that life naturally takes care of itself and the struggle eases.

Defining surrender

Surrender is release. It is giving up all that is to a higher power, without regard for outcome. Surrender is a step beyond acceptance because it requires you not only to see the situation accurately and accept what is but then to turn over all your thoughts and angst and attachment surrounding your circumstance to the universal source. Instead of trying to change or control outcomes, you trust in the divine order of the universe to take care of things. You surrender to God, trusting that you'll be given the strength to handle whatever does happen.

Key idea

When you surrender, you give up your worries to a higher power without expectation of any particular outcome.

When you surrender, you are giving up the need for things to be a certain way. You are giving up the need to know what is going to happen. You are giving up your desire to control. You are detaching from your desire to keep everything the same. You trust that, however things end up, they will be just as they should be. You are giving up the fight and making a commitment to live with what is – even if it's not what you most desire.

The ancient practice of *Isvara Pranidhana*

More than 1,700 years ago, the author of the Yoga Sutras – thought to be the Indian yogi Patanjali – wrote about *Isvara Pranidhana*, translated from Sanskrit to mean 'giving up our actions to God'.

This act of 'giving up' requires us to operate with personal integrity and right-minded action, according to Patanjali. It demands that we do our best and then give our control and our desire for a particular outcome to a higher power. Patanjali believed surrender was a choice available to anyone who trusts in the absolute order of the universe and accepts that life is a composite of easy and difficult moments, joys and sadnesses, births and deaths.

Try it now

Think of a time when you chose – or were forced – to give up on something you desired. Write it down in your journal and for a moment feel how much you wanted things to be different. Then write down one positive thing that came out of that surrender. When we let go, we make space for new things to come in, and this leads to growth.

SURRENDER IS ACTIVE

Of course, this doesn't mean you relish or enjoy every moment. We are often pushed to surrender during times of great turmoil because nothing we've done has helped and we don't know what else to do. Surrender allows you to shift your focus from trying to create an outcome to deeply accepting any outcome. Instead of fighting against what might happen, you begin living with what is.

Key idea

When you surrender, you give up your worry, stress, concern and thoughts about what might be, and deal, instead, with what is.

For example, if you're facing a grave diagnosis, surrendering to the situation doesn't mean you give up or stop medical treatment. Nor does it mean deluding yourself with thoughts of death or even survival. What surrender does is help you to accept whatever comes without despair or stress or struggle. It allows you to give up all that fear and anger to something beyond what we can see, so that you can live fully now.

Remember this

Surrender is also a powerful way to engage and awaken to life during the good times. Often, even when we're having a peak experience, there is a part of us that worries about the goodness coming to an end. Of course it will. But instead of holding on so tight, surrender to the moment. Enjoy it thoroughly. Experience it fully. Embrace it and allow it to go.

Our ability to practise surrender will be tested time and time again, through the small frustrations of daily life as well as during major life transitions. Even when we're solidly on our path of spiritual self-discovery, setbacks such as death, illness, poverty and disappointments challenge our spiritual ideals and practices.

It is tough to think about surrendering to our grief over the death of a loved one, or over the loss of our health, or over the end of our most valued relationship. There is nothing about these things that we like. It is our ego's instinct to keep us from pain, and therefore we fight and resist in an effort to avoid the discomfort that enters our lives. But it comes anyway. It is often during these times of great strife that we can find peace in surrender. This takes practice and commitment. Surrender is not a passive process.

Case study: Amy

Spirituality has been the link that has helped Amy, a writer, stay emotionally, physically, and mentally healthy. Having that connection and a faith in something greater than herself has helped her handle life stresses that have included a hostile divorce, her son's difficulties with mental illness and addiction, and her own anxiety issues. Her spiritual development, though, began as a search.

'I was looking for more meaning in my life,' Amy says. 'I had a lot of "things", but my life felt empty despite the possessions and outward markings of success.'

Now Amy spends time in prayer and meditation every evening before bed and on waking in the morning. She also finds inspiration by reading the Bible and books on meditation. These practices have helped her to be more honest in her life and to learn to surrender to what is.

'One goal of my spirituality is to let go of my will, which tends to get me into trouble, and focus on God's will for my life,' says Amy. 'For me, it would be very difficult to grow as a person without a regular spiritual practice in my life. I'm always trying to improve my spiritual practices and awareness, with the goal of developing a closer relationship with God.'

Try it now

Pick a situation in your life right now. Evaluate it. What is working, and what is not? Now simply consider what your life would feel like if you gave up your attachment or thoughts about this situation. You don't have to do it; just consider what it would be like to not have to worry about how things might turn out. Imagine how it would feel to do nothing but let go of the anxiety. Notice that the tension in your body changes when you simply think about letting this go. Learning to surrender requires practice, and it starts by noticing what it feels like to let up a little bit. Write in your journal about these questions and feelings.

PEACE IS POSSIBLE

The act of letting go and giving up your worries to God activates your faith, challenges your ego and pushes you towards clarity and self-realization. It is a tremendous relief when you are able to acknowledge that you don't have all the answers and that you can turn over your troubles to a higher energy.

This act allows you to access peace and joy at any time – even in the midst of heartache. When you are not hung up on outcomes or expectations, you aren't dependent on external responses to be happy. Despite the pain, you can choose to feel peaceful because you know, on a deep level, that there is a reason for everything. This state of surrendering to the moment also helps you stay open to and aware of any insights that emerge.

Key idea

When you give up the struggle through surrender, your attention shifts to the present and your awareness expands to draw meaning from all of life. This helps insight emerge, even during painful times.

When you surrender, you give up your need to know why and mute your compulsion to understand. Instead, you know that the knowledge you seek will appear when it's most needed. This adds meaning to your life.

When we give up our attachments to outcome, we often create a spiritual space, leaving room for whatever comes. That can illuminate the blessings that are behind the challenge. How many times have you suffered a great disappointment or deep anxiety, only to realize after the moment had passed, or you surrendered to it, that within the struggle there were also powerful gifts?

Here are some situations where surrender can lead to meaningful insight.

▶ Lessons learned through a painful divorce helped create a healthy relationship with your soulmate.

▶ A job loss provided an opportunity to pursue a dream career.

▶ An illness taught compassion and forgiveness that helped restore relationships with loved ones.

Try it now

Think of a problem or worry that is plaguing you, something you're holding on to tightly. Set the intention now to give it up. Take a deep breath and repeat this phrase: 'Now I release all my fears and anxieties and despair to the higher power, trusting that the wisdom I need will be illuminated along my path.'

Then, as you exhale, imagine all the worries and fears being blown out and up into the hands of the universal source. Feel the relief. Feel yourself open to whatever is next.

How surrender springs from faith

Faith is the belief in something bigger than what you see and what you cognitively understand. It's the deep-rooted knowing that there is a higher consciousness and that it operates in your life even on those days when you don't know how it works – even on those days when you doubt that it is there at all.

Without faith, surrender is difficult. But, surrender can cultivate faith. The act of giving up your challenge to a higher power – of relinquishing control – can free you up to live from a more spiritually resonate place and help you experience moments of awakening that otherwise would go unnoticed.

Four ways to cultivate faith

The best way to nourish your faith is to notice how spirit is already working in your life. It's easier to connect to our higher consciousness, easier to rely on it, when we have evidence of its power. Your job, then, is to go looking, to become aware of the mysteries in your life, to embrace what comes your way, and to notice that you are an essential part of the fabric of it all.

Key idea

Faith isn't something that you either have or don't have. It is a choice: one that requires attention. It must be cultivated and protected. A daily spiritual practice can help reconnect you to the quiet space inside you where spirit resides. Mindful attention can help you see the practical ways source energy works in your life. Reflecting on these things can help build trust that there is a higher energy guiding us.

A practical approach to building faith starts by noticing, and then using these other strategies to stay connected to your faith.

1   **Remember the good from the bad.** We tend to trust the universe more when we see that our most troubled times yielded some of the greatest gifts or lessons. Certainly, you don't need to go looking for trouble. You may never welcome it in. Acceptance can sometimes be slow in coming, but the rough spots will come anyhow. Find solace in knowing that there is something to be gained even if you don't know what that is yet. To do this, practise. Think back to a previous hard time five or ten years ago and remember one good thing that evolved from that moment. Trust that it will happen again.

2   **Become aware of the perfection of all things.** Stare at the stars, watch the ocean waves roll in, hike through the mountains and see that the stars still appear and the waves keep rolling, even despite great adversity. We are not

separate from the source that created all this so, of course, we are included in the flow of a dynamic universe. Just because something is uncomfortable or painful doesn't mean it's flawed. The experiences of your life – both the good and the bad – are there to serve you. There is perfection in that.

3 **Take action.** Developing trust in the things we cannot see requires devotion. Giving ourselves over to a power that we don't fully understand requires strength. You can cultivate both of those things. Read inspirational material, talk to spiritual people, seek answers to your biggest questions, play with your intuition and simply notice what comes into your life. By surrounding ourselves with stories of faith, we begin to find a way to live a more faithful life in our own way.

4 **Become aware of all that you don't know.** We live with the illusion that we know the best plan for our lives, or that we alone contain all the wisdom we need to function in this world. That is not true. Nor do we need all the answers to thrive. Be open to what you don't know. Identify your doubts. Explore them, but don't judge them. Just notice what they are, see what questions emerge, ask for answers, and take note of the people, songs, books and insights that come into your life. They often hold illuminating information. You will find that you receive the answers you need when the time is right – whether you like it or not.

RECOGNIZING FAITH

Faith and surrender are inextricably related. When you recognize that there is nothing left to do or fix, when you are tired of the fight, you can give up the struggle in an instant by surrendering to it. This is an act of faith because it requires you to give up what you think you know to something intangible.

Surrender often also means disconnecting from something you desperately wanted. In this moment of letting go, you drop the notion that you know what's best and trust that higher consciousness will guide you in the direction you must go next.

Faith is trust. It is acceptance to the deepest degree and it's an active way to unite with the universal source. Only by giving up our struggle to a higher power do we embrace wholeheartedly our relationship with God.

Remember this

Surrender requires practice. Next time you're feeling overwhelmed, make a list of all that you feel must be done. Then pick out only the top three essential chores and let the others go. Notice that nothing falls apart. You don't have to do it all. You can let things go, let up a bit, and life will continue.

STEPS TO SURRENDER

As you cultivate faith, surrender also becomes easier. However, when you cast off your worries to some higher force, you are not necessarily going to see big changes and you won't always feel better. Sometimes there is immediate relief and peace, either brief or enduring. At other times you sense no change at all. Nevertheless, you always benefit by making a conscious choice to release your struggles to a higher power. The act of doing this causes a shift in your awareness and thought patterns. Your thoughts are no longer a single perspective. You now operate from awareness, inclusive of a greater source.

With surrender, you acknowledge the situation and then turn it over to something greater. You no longer have to single-handedly change or fix or handle the challenge. Instead, you move into the moment with deep acceptance, and then you move through it.

Three of the things we've already studied in this book – acceptance, awareness and belief in a higher power – can aid in the act of surrender. Combined with the other elements mentioned here, they can help you let go of your pain and move beyond it.

1 **Accept what is.** See the truth, without being hindered by belief or desires, and accept it deeply.

2 **Trust in a higher energy.** When you know that you don't have the answers or are no longer clear on what to do, trust that there is a force that can guide you through it. You don't have to worry that you aren't enough – you will discover that you are.

3 **Embrace all of life.** Even in moments of great despair and heartache, there can be great joy and possibility. Embrace every moment, knowing that it will yield the insight you need to awaken to the next phase of your life. Love what is before you. Be grateful for it. When you are busy trying to create a specific outcome, you miss out on the moments of life *now*.

4 **Find something that's real for you and focus on that.** The ocean waves will continue to roll. The sun rises each day, whether you see it or not. The natural energy of the universe continues without your management. You can surrender to the dawn of the day. You can trust in that. Start with what you can see and touch, and recognize that these amazing things happen whether you know how they work or not. This is how faith works.

5 **Release it, and move on.** When you have fully accepted your situation, and released your attachment to outcome, it's time to offer it up to God. Make the offering through a verbal statement or write it down, so you're really clear that now is the time to surrender.

▷ Say it out loud: 'Today I turn over my fear and stress and concern over this [state the situation] to a higher power. I surrender to you and thank you for taking it from me. I am now free to become present to the other moments of my life.'

▷ Breathe deeply while doing this, to ease fear and stress. Then sit quietly for a moment and allow the energy to shift.

6 **Remember the surrender.** Now that you've given it over to God, you may find your mind coming back to the circumstance and reattaching or worrying all over again. That's common. When that happens, gently remind yourself that you have given away that worry, and move on to something that feels better.

7 **Take positive right action.** Now move into the next moment of your life. You are free to love deeply again, to learn and grow and have fun. After you've cast off your worry and

surrendered your stress, take one step in a different, good-feeling direction.

It is only by taking these steps that we can participate fully in this life experience. Until we surrender, we are stagnant: replaying our troubles, wrestling with our pain and working to control outcomes – just hoping we can grab what we desire.

By letting go of our need to control and manipulate our circumstances, by relinquishing our need for certain results, we take the pressure off and create a new space of possibility.

HOW EGO GETS IN OUR WAY

Of course, one of the biggest barriers to surrender that we encounter is our ego. It's there, trying to shield us from pain, by telling us that we must get busy to solve our problems. In surrender, you silence the ego by reminding it that all is unfolding as it is supposed to. You are safe and guided by a more powerful force. Ultimately, you see the ego's chatter simply as noise. There is nothing scary about surrender. It is liberating.

Try it now

Often we are afraid to give up control because we feel we must manage or worry to make things happen. This is our ego talking. Right now, consider something that's causing you stress. Write down exactly what your inner voices are saying, sentence by sentence. Now – sentence by sentence – read the words aloud, scrutinizing and exposing them for their untruths by finding evidence to the contrary. If the fear remains, release it to the universe and move on.

FOLLOW THE ENERGY

Ultimately, spiritual growth depends on the energy you choose to follow. You can choose to go with worry and the need to hold on, suppress and control, or you can go with the energy of creativity, expansion and possibility. These are fuelled by love and compassion and they move fast. They're expansive and capable of helping you find joy and peace despite pain and stress.

The act of surrender opens up mental and spiritual space, leaving room for any possibility. It is also a chance for you to reaffirm your spiritual commitment because it requires you to trust in something unseen, but something that exists just the same – God, or source energy, or higher consciousness.

You can hang on to the struggle or surrender to it, allowing yourself to align with the universal source and create a space for peace, gratitude and other good things to come.

Focus points

✳ Surrender means to give up the need for control and certainty to a higher power, no matter what the outcome.

✳ The act of surrender eases suffering and leads to greater peace because it requires you to give up the fight and struggle and accept what is.

✳ Faith and surrender are inextricably connected. When you surrender, you are affirming your faith and strengthening your spiritual connection.

✳ Both faith and surrender are active endeavours and can be cultivated with practice and attention.

✳ The ego is a barrier to surrender but, by acknowledging those inner voices and disputing them, you learn that surrender is not scary or passive, but liberating.

Next step

When we detach from every outcome, we are free to engage in life from a more peaceful place. This process of surrender can be made easier through contemplation, meditation and moments of solitude that allow us to gain insight. In the next chapter we'll explore the importance of solitude to spiritual practice and explain how to get quiet through meditation and contemplation.

9

Getting quiet

In this chapter you will learn:

▶ *why time for quiet and solitude is essential to spiritual practice*
▶ *the value of contemplation*
▶ *practical guidelines for contemplation*
▶ *how to use the centring prayer*
▶ *what effect meditation has on our physical and spiritual health*
▶ *different styles of meditation.*

Self-assessment: How good are you at getting quiet?

Quiet time alone is a real treat for some people but a trial for others. Answer the following questions to find out how good you are at getting quiet.

1 When faced with an unexpected night alone at home, what do you do?

  a Spend time surfing the web

  b Sit in the quiet and write in your journal or read

  c Call all the friends you rarely have time to talk to

2 What is contemplation?

  a Thinking about how to solve the problems in your life

  b Focused thought on spiritual things as a form of learning and devotion

  c Pondering your goals

3 When you have nothing scheduled, what do you feel?

  a That you must find things to do and rush around and get it all done

  b Relief and peace

  c Lonely

4 What is meditation?

  a A practice that is difficult to learn without professional guidance

  b A practice that involves focused attention

  c Something that can only be done while sitting still, with legs crossed

5 What is solitude?

  a Rarely a productive time

  b A chance for creativity to flourish

  c Boring

6 To experience any true benefit, for how long must you meditate?

  a For an hour a day

  b For just a few minutes a day

  c Every morning and evening

7 When you get quiet, what do you notice?

  a How dirty the windows are

  b Your intuition providing helpful information

  c How relaxed you feel

8 When you are feeling most stressed, how do you cope?

  a By trying to get everything done so you can move on with your life

  b By taking a deep breath and sitting quietly for five minutes

  c By eating junk food

9 What prevents you taking regular time for quiet and solitude?

  a Life is too busy to sit still and meditate

  b The inability to schedule time for it each day

  c It's a waste of time since nothing gets done

10 What do you do when you think of spending a day by yourself?

  a Feel nervous and aren't sure what to do

  b Feel excited and set aside some of that time for quiet study or thought

  c Plan a party and start calling all your friends

What did you discover?

Mostly **a** answers imply that you are someone who feels they have to be doing and producing to be successful in life. You will certainly get a lot done, but will you be working on the things that matter most? In everyday life, moments of quiet can help you gain valuable insight that will keep you on purpose and on your spiritual path.

Mostly **b** answers indicate that you already know the value of solitude and contemplation. Your greatest challenge may be to find time to do it during days filled with work and family demands. Surprisingly, when you set the intention, you can find little pockets of quiet to help in your practice.

Mostly **c** answers show that you thrive in social situations and the thought of time alone may be frightening. You don't have to become a recluse to benefit from a few minutes of quiet each day. Experiment with it. Build in some of the practices described below for at least 30 days and you'll find yourself more aware and in tune with yourself and others during social situations.

Finding time

The basis of all spiritual practice is to help you know yourself and your connection to God in a practical and tangible way. To live a spiritual life, then, is to create time and space to do the things that help you awaken to your higher consciousness. Awareness, acceptance and presence are all states of being and practices that can connect you to the divine, but they are also practical exercises to help you live better on this earth.

It's often the noise of our lives that prevents us from becoming aware. Life's demands and its incessant hum and pace are what keep us from getting quiet. Until we learn to sit quietly with ourselves, our lives will be reactive and tense.

It is hard to know God when you do not know yourself. It is a challenge to become aware when you are bombarded by the unconscious noise of television and phones and gossip. It is nearly impossible to accept what is if you are distracted by all that isn't – the superfluous sounds of our culture and the inner voices of ourselves.

It's time to get quiet. It's time to settle in with yourself, to spend time in contemplation to learn what you think, to explore meditation to free your mind, to grow comfortable in solitude. This isn't as alarming as it sounds.

Quiet and solitude ease the stress of modern life

We have become accustomed to operating at a frenetic pace. Technology connects us anywhere, any time, in fractions of a second. We are surrounded constantly by noise – the hum of the computer, sounds of passing cars, music on the radio, the computer and the phone. We are constantly accessible, if we choose to be. People can reach us via mobile phone, Skype or video conferencing, even when we are on holiday. It's no wonder that many of us are feeling overwhelmed, stressed and fatigued. It's no surprise that anxiety-related disorders are on the rise.

It's becoming harder to cope with the pressures because the noise of modern life makes it hard to connect to our spiritual side. Spirituality is a way of life, accessible in any moment, but it thrives in moments of quiet when we can acutely notice our thoughts.

The more time we spend in solitude, in contemplation or meditation, the better we become at managing daily pressures. During quiet moments, we learn to observe our thoughts and focus our attention in a way that yields profound spiritual insight and in a way that helps us handle the chaos that threatens to overtake our lives.

Try it now

Close your eyes and for two minutes pay attention to the sounds in and around you. When we are constantly exposed to internal and external noise – whether it is from an iPod or our own inner voice – it's hard to connect with our spiritual nature. In fact, we tend to tune out the noise but it continues to distract and stress us on an unconscious level.

Part of getting quiet is to become aware and conscious of the noise that is always running below the surface of our lives. When we turn the volume down, we can appreciate the silence and be open to what we discover there.

GETTING QUIET WITHIN AND WITHOUT

It's not enough to turn off the radio or shut down the phone. There needs to be an internal shift as well. Turn off the noise in your environment and quiet your inner thoughts. To do that, you've got to find moments to slow down, to allow yourself room to be in the space you are without expectation or demand. You've got to escape from the chaos that you create.

Remember this

Feeling overwhelmed? Find a spot to be alone for even just five minutes. Whether it's your car, a bathroom, your office with the door closed or an empty conference room, turn off the noise so you can tune into yourself.

CHAOS COMES FROM UNCONSCIOUSNESS

A busy life can cause us to be reactive. It contributes to an even busier mind. We often set about doing things without even realizing all that we are doing. We mindlessly cross things off from our to-do lists; we often don't sit down for meals or even remember what we eat; and we talk on the phone while doing other tasks. We hurry to get things done so that we can fall into bed and rest for a few hours before starting again.

When we are living like this, we're unconscious. Life feels chaotic. With too much to process we try to take control, manage and, again, find ourselves moving away from acceptance and surrender and any deepening connection to source.

SOLITUDE IS NOT LONELINESS

Solitude is a way to silence the internal and external environmental noise. But this is not loneliness. Solitude is an engaged state. It is time that you give to yourself to learn who you are, to appreciate life just as it is. It is a chance to revitalize and reconnect with our deepest desires and our higher consciousness.

Loneliness implies lack. It feels as though you're missing something and it comes when there is a forced aloneness. Solitude that springs from loneliness feels empty and depressing rather than insightful and engaging.

There is a way out of loneliness if you reach out and participate in this world. But the best way to deal with the noise of life is to get quiet and take time alone.

Key idea

Loneliness implies that something is missing from your life. Solitude is an active state, where you enjoy time alone as a way of developing clarity, peace and insight. If you are feeling lonely and isolated from others, you can begin to cultivate new friendships. Solitude, which gives you room to know your own thoughts, can be cultivated too, by scheduling it in.

Remember this

Social connection is essential to our health and wellbeing, but it's up to you to reach out to others. If you are feeling lonely, explore your passions and do the things that you most love to do. Take a class, sign up to volunteer, join a gym and connect with others through social media. Meeting people through shared interests is a good way to develop new relationships.

TAKING TIME OUT

Solitude appears in many different ways. It can be inspiring and re-energizing, whether you have a few moments to yourself to watch a waterfall, an hour to read or paint, or five minutes in the car before the school pick-up. Praying alone in church is helpful to some. For others, sitting in contemplation is powerful.

No matter how you do it, it's valuable to build quiet moments into each day. Become aware, too, of the opportunities for quiet time that naturally present themselves during the transitions that happen throughout the day.

For example, take a few minutes after the children have gone to school to sit quietly with your thoughts before heading to work. Perhaps you can get up 20 minutes earlier than everyone else to have some alone time. Maybe your partner is late getting home from work and, instead of tackling household chores, you could take that moment for quiet reflection.

Use these unexpected opportunities for quiet, but be sure to schedule time for solitude and other spiritual practices like contemplation too.

CONTEMPLATING THE BIG QUESTIONS

Mystics and seekers alike often spend time in contemplation. During this time of focused attention, many heighten their awareness of God by reading inspired passages and by reflecting on questions that arise.

Contemplation leaves space for the questions simply to be asked. You create an environment that allows you to investigate your thoughts and discover your own truths. The answers may not be immediate; the questions are not always easily resolved. However, when you are in quiet contemplation, you are learning and the practice is often as important as any of the answers you get.

In time, you will discover the wisdom you seek. Then you can investigate the answers through contemplative practice. In this way, contemplation helps us unearth the layers of false beliefs, egoist patterns, fears, attachments and judgments until all that remains is clarity of mind.

Basic guidelines for contemplation

1 Sit in a comfortable position. Turn off the phone and computer and minimize any noise or external disturbances.

2 Take some deep breaths and notice the air moving in and out of your lungs.

3 Begin to observe your thoughts without judgment.

4 Reflect on a question or belief: *What am I? What is my purpose? What do I need to know?* Any other big-life question can be useful in contemplation.

5 Think about the answers that arise. Notice the other questions that come up, but stay focused on the question you started with.

6 As insights are revealed, gently question them. *Are they true? Are they relevant? Are they helpful?*

7 Continue to explore your thoughts during daily contemplative time.

Try it now

Come up with a question – something you want to understand better in your life, or something with a spiritual arc. Ask it out loud and spend five minutes quietly thinking about it. Don't judge the insights you receive; just notice them. Then spend a couple of minutes investigating what you learned. Did you receive information that can help resolve your questions? Did you gain insight that prompted more inquiry?

After about five minutes, go back to whatever you were doing before. Allow the question to remain in the background. Notice what comes up, but don't focus any special attention on it.

At the end of the day, note in your journal anything that occurred that conveyed unique insight about the question you were contemplating.

LIVING WITH WHAT YOU LEARN

Some teachers recommend that you pick a particular spiritual topic or question to contemplate each day, as part of your spiritual exploration. You can begin your contemplative practice by reading about the topic, going deep into the material and questioning it by asking:

▶ Is it true?

▶ Does it matter to me?

▶ How does it impact others?

If it is true, and the practice or knowledge seems relevant to your life, you can then start living with it. This contemplative style requires time and discipline. Sometimes you'll sit in quiet contemplation and apparently gain no new information at all. Devote yourself to the practice, though, because in time you will reach a deeper understanding, one that will move you along the enlightened path.

WRITING YOUR THOUGHTS

Writing about your thoughts and insights is another way of establishing a contemplative practice. Pose the question on the page, and out loud too if you like. Before you begin writing, just let the question sit there for a moment.

Begin to notice insights emerging and, as they come, write them out on the page. When you've finished writing, go back to the words and study, challenge or question them. Which ones resonate? Do you now have a deeper understanding of a question? If not, that's okay. Understanding and clarity can feel slow to come. They rarely unveil themselves until we are ready. So be patient and continue contemplating these questions over the following weeks and months.

CONTEMPLATION: THE INTERSECT BETWEEN INTELLECT AND SPIRIT

Contemplation is both a spiritual and an intellectual exercise. We ask a question, analyse information, consider our thoughts, study other perspectives and go within for deeper insights until we reach some greater understanding of the matter at hand. When we contemplate, we are not allowing our thoughts to run away with us, but we are directing them with conscious attention. When we gain some knowledge or wisdom on the topic or the question posed, it resonates with our spiritual selves and we experience clarity or a sense of knowing.

This can feel like an epiphany, a sudden intuition, a moment of awakening or instant understanding. Still, it evolved out of quiet contemplation and inquiry.

Key idea

Contemplation is a practice that allows the mind and spirit to merge. You pose the question or introduce the thought through spiritual awareness, and then investigate what comes. This is a way to access the wisdom of higher consciousness.

Remember this

Next time you're feeling off balance or overwhelmed, look for the quiet spaces within the noise. Quiet rests beautifully between musical notes, giving music its structure. It's the silent charge before the thunder. Find the silence between spoken words and look for the silence you always hold within. This little exercise will shift your focus from the busy chaos of life to the peace that is always there too.

Prayer is the conversation

Unlike contemplation, where you go within to find the answers, prayer is a direct communication with the divine. This can happen in the middle of a busy moment or in the quiet moments of solitude that you find in your day.

Prayer does not have to be beseeching. You can speak to your God at any point, in gratitude and praise, or about any topic as you would with a friend. How you pray matters less than the intention and motivation that the prayer comes from, says Father Thomas Keating, a spiritual leader and Trappist monk who has cultivated the practice of the **centring prayer**.

THE MEDITATIVE, CONTEMPLATIVE ASPECTS OF PRAYER

The centring prayer is a contemplative and meditative practice in the Christian tradition where you choose a sacred word like Jesus, Mother, Peace, Spirit or Divine. The word is often received after reciting a short prayer asking for inspiration from the divine. Then, with your word in mind, you sit comfortably, eyes closed, and focus on this word for about 20 minutes.

The word symbolizes your openness to God's presence and divine action within. As you silently focus your attention on that word, become aware of any other thoughts that enter and gently shift your mind back to the sacred word.

Case study: Paul

'Spiritual practices gave me strength when I had none of my own,' writes Paul, a parish pastor who meditates and uses the centring prayer as part of his daily routine.

Paul learned the centring prayer several years ago, while participating in a businessmen's Bible study group. He was so compelled by what he learned through the prayer and his studies that he wanted to share it with others, so he became an ordained minister.

The centering prayer and other practices help Paul stay centred, peaceful and calm, no matter what life throws at him. It's also given him deeper awareness of his own thoughts.

'I'm in greater control of sorting through the barrage of thoughts that flow through my mind during the day and I'm able to choose the ones that I want to follow, letting go of the negative thoughts that, if allowed to persist, gain greater influence,' says Paul. 'The practice helps remind me to live in the present moment and stop running into the future to deal with problems that may never happen anyway.'

Paul says his spiritual exploration has also led to deeper insights and new meanings that have enhanced his understanding of Scripture. He can now tune into what he calls the voice of God. Instead of reacting to the opinions and views of others, he has greater clarity to understand his own.

'My spiritual practices have helped me to pay attention to how I am internally reacting and responding to external situations. Awareness of self allows me to see that my actions are often stimulated by emotions, and if I want to understand the actions that I don't want to repeat, then I need to explore what I value that needs to be protected or defended in a way... Then I can objectively decide if that value is worth protecting.'

Meditation leads to physical and spiritual health

While contemplation – the exploration of a particular idea – can be a part of daily meditation, and prayer can help foster the direct connection to the divine, the goal of many meditation practices is to clear the mind of mental chatter altogether. Emptying the mind and freeing it from ideas, judgments, worries and thoughts helps you become fully conscious and awakened to all that you are as a spiritual, physical and mental being. In this state, you can experience not only great clarity but also serenity, insight and unity with God, or higher consciousness.

The benefits of regular meditation are profound when it comes to spiritual development. Thousands of studies show that people who meditate regularly also experience significant physical benefits including fewer illnesses and greater wellbeing.

Regular meditation increases brain activity and can alter the physical structure of the brain in a way that has prolonged benefits. One study from the University of California in Los Angeles shows that a consistent practice can even reduce 'age-related brain atrophy'. Meditators also experience pain differently – they don't notice their pain as much – and they record lower blood pressure, greater immune function and relief from dozens of other physical and mental health symptoms.

MEDITATION DOESN'T HAVE TO BE HARD

Many people are wary of meditating because they don't know how to do it properly or they claim not to have the time to sit. Others try it, only to find that it's tough to sit quietly for 20 minutes and focus their thoughts – so they give up after a couple of attempts.

If you've ever used one of these excuses, then they alone are precisely the reason you should be meditating. If it's too hard to quiet your thoughts and connect with self, meditation is the answer. It doesn't have to be hard.

To get started, follow these basic guidelines and you'll soon experience the spiritual awakening and physical benefits that everyone is talking about. And you don't have to be a monk or yogi to experience them!

▶ **Basic meditation guidelines**

1 **Find a quiet place and sit.** Choose a set amount of time for your meditation. If you're the unsettled type, programme an alarm to go off at the end so you aren't continuously

fighting to look at a clock. Then, get comfortable. You don't need to be cross-legged on the floor. It's best to be upright, straight-backed in a comfortable chair. You can have your hands at your sides along the armrests or resting in your lap, palms up, with index fingers touching, or with palms flat on your thighs. The key is to get into a comfortable, yet alert position.

2 **Begin with your breath.** Take a slow, deep breath in through your nose and exhale through your mouth. Focused breathing is an aspect of many meditation practices and fundamental to spiritual development. It is a way to connect your spirit to your mind and body and to centre yourself. In fact, the word 'breath' itself is derived from the Latin word 'spiritus', which also means life.

> 'Breathing is a bridge between mind and body, the connection between consciousness and unconsciousness and the movement of spirit in matter.'
>
> Dr Andrew Weil, holistic physician and author

Try it now

Sit up straight, feet on the floor. Take a deep, slow breath in through your nose and exhale slowly through your mouth. Do this ten times, paying attention to your breath. Notice how you feel. Deep, slow, rhythmic breathing can change our physiology, helping us regulate our moods, replacing fear and our fight-or-flight response with keen awareness and focus. Balance and tranquillity are also restored in the process.

3 **Be still with whatever comes.** Now that you have reached some calm through your deep breathing, be still for whatever length of time you've chosen. Don't worry about following some prescribed rules or about reaching a certain state of peace or consciousness. Just be in the moment with whatever thoughts or sensations arise. Don't cling to any one thought; notice it, and let it move out. Be mindful. Don't judge. Just let the process take on a natural flow.

CREATING THE PRACTICE

Once you have worked with the basic guidelines above, it's important to make time for a daily practice. A regular 20-minute practice twice a day, or a half-hour session once a day, can be effective, but even short periods of five or ten minutes at a time can be helpful.

It's essential, though, that you meditate daily for at least 30 days. If it feels difficult at first, if you notice your mind wandering and your body growing restless, that's okay and part of the process. Like anything else, we must develop a habit of sitting. It's not something most of us do naturally, so it's unsettling in the beginning. However, with practice and repetition, it becomes easier and more rewarding to do.

Key idea

It may feel difficult to sit still and meditate every day. Your life is consumed by so much activity. We are simply unfamiliar with being still and quiet. To support our spiritual growth, we must create a new habit of quiet. If you commit to a regular meditation practice for at least 30 days, you'll begin to replace the habits that keep you busy and unconscious with those that support your spiritual growth and restore peace and balance in your life.

Types of meditation

Once you begin the basics of meditation practice and set aside time each day to sit, you may be ready to learn, or at least experiment with, some of the dozens of meditation techniques being practised around the world. They nearly all involve a focus on the breath and a shift to present-moment awareness. Quieting and focusing the mind is also an aspect of all meditation, but each offers a different way of doing it.

Meditation is sometimes classified into two forms. The first, called the concentrative style, means you meditate or focus your thoughts on your breath or a specific mental image, a mantra or an object such as a religious icon. Contemplation can also be a concentrative form. Concentrative meditation techniques can be effective in developing your focus and attention. Non-concentrative meditation styles are a less focused form of meditation and can help broaden your awareness, often using movement.

No matter how you meditate, the practice will help you gain clarity, peace and focus over your thoughts.

CONCENTRATIVE MEDITATION

▶ Mantra meditation

A mantra is a phrase or word or sound that you repeat aloud or to yourself over and over throughout the duration of the meditation session, and even at times throughout the day. Your focus stays on this mantra throughout. It can help support your growth in a specific way, and the repetition works to quiet the mind from all distraction.

Spiritual mantras often declare the name of God in some way. Other mantras evoke a virtuous quality that you'd like consciously to develop in your own life, such as patience or peace or love. Still others focus on a particular vibration or frequency like 'Ohm', which is used to connect to the energies of higher consciousness.

Many people choose their own mantra by selecting phrases or tones containing words that are significant, inspiring or powerful for them. Repetition of the mantra is key in this form of meditation, practitioners say.

▶ Transcendental meditation

This is a form of mantra meditation where participants receive specific training and a mantra from the TM organization. Some say this form can only be learned from designated teachers.

▶ Breathing meditation

This is popular because it can be done anywhere for as little as five minutes as well as for an extended time. To try out this form, simply get quiet, get comfortable, and inhale and exhale slowly while keeping your attention focused on your breath. If your thoughts wander, bring them back to your breath.

Try it now

Use meditation to ease the stress of the moment. Set your alarm for five minutes. Close your eyes and take three slow, deep breaths, inhaling through your nose and exhaling through your mouth.

Now imagine your problem or stressful situation and, with each breath out, focus on the word peace blowing the problem out of your consciousness. You no longer have to hold on to it. Now shift your awareness to the word peace and imagine it filling the space in and around you. When your alarm rings, take a deep breath and open your eyes.

NON-CONCENTRATIVE MEDITATION

▶ **Mindfulness meditation**

This is a meditation style where you get quiet, observe your thoughts and become aware of any sensations. You are a witness to all that is around and within. You don't cling to your ideas; you don't judge them or attach meaning to them. Instead, you simply notice them, and let them go.

Jon Kabat-Zinn, founding Executive Director of the Center for Mindfulness in Medicine, Health Care, and Society at the University of Massachusetts Medical School, says that when we give space to our thoughts without manipulation or judgment, we are able to gain clarity and understanding that can help us better cope with stress and tap into intuitive insights.

▶ **Walking or moving meditation**

Moving meditation is a form of meditation gaining popularity. It can be practised either in a concentrated way with attention to a particular movement or in a broader, more mindful way. During walking meditation you walk or run, paying careful attention to specific body parts such as the feel of your feet hitting the ground. You empty your mind of all thoughts except for that particular sensation. You do this in silence, so turn off that MP3 player.

You can also take a non-concentrated approach by simply watching the thoughts and sensations you experience as you walk, but staying clear of the distractions of rumination and worry. Each time you notice your thoughts stray, you bring them back to the present.

With other forms of moving meditation practice, some meditators sit and sway or move their arms or other body parts in a rhythmic motion while repeating a mantra or sitting in silence. Their attention always stays on the movement.

▶ **Yoga and t'ai chi**

These activities can also be done as meditation practice. They require you to focus your attention while completing slow, rhythmic movements.

Key idea

Meditation can heighten your life experience by helping you hone your concentration, balance your energies and align and awaken to higher consciousness. A regular meditation practice doesn't have to feel daunting. Even five or ten minutes a day in breathing meditation can have great benefits.

CARVING OUT TIME FOR QUIET

Whether you spend time in meditation or contemplation, whether you keep a journal, sit mindfully or pray, solitude is essential to spiritual growth. When we surround ourselves with quiet aloneness in our external world, we can focus more deeply on our internal world and awaken to higher consciousness and greater physical and spiritual health.

If you're not ready to embark on a regular meditation practice, or you find yourself intimidated by the questions sparked by quiet contemplation, start a casual practice of quiet solitude and see where it leads you.

▶ **Create quiet time**

Each day, create ten minutes of quiet time. Turn off the television and MP3 player, escape from the other noise of your life and simply be still with no other objective than just to hear the quiet. Find time between the duties of your day. Take a minute of quiet inactivity in the shower. Pause for a few moments before you get out of the car and run into the house after work. Take on a quiet household chore like weeding or folding laundry by yourself and just move into the silence.

Note in your journal any insights that arise during these times, or any uncertainties and discomfort. Getting quiet may take some getting used to. But when you become aware of the wisdom within the quiet, you'll be more likely to establish a regular practice.

Focus points

* Solitude is an essential practice to shut out the noise of life, so that you can go within to heighten your awareness, discover your spirituality, and ease the stress of daily life.
* Contemplation, which is the quiet focus, study and investigation of specific questions or thoughts, is a way to develop personal and spiritual understanding and clarity.
* Prayer is a direct discourse with the divine.
* Meditation, the practice of observing the mind and expanding consciousness, is another way to restore health and peace and grow spiritually.
* An ongoing practice of solitude, in any of its forms, will ease stress, promote health and wellbeing, enhance creativity and nourish your spiritual growth and awareness.

Next step

One of the most restorative ways to experience solitude is within nature. More and more people are doing this to enhance their spiritual growth. We are all connected: what we do influences our environment and, in turn, ourselves. In the next chapter we'll look at how tapping into the natural energies of the universe can inspire our own actualization.

10

Finding balance in the natural world

In this chapter you will learn:

- *how nature can help you deepen your spirituality*
- *what ecopsychology means*
- *practical ways to reconnect with the natural world*
- *how nature heals and expands our spiritual awareness.*

Self-assessment: What role does the natural world play in your life?

Take this true/false quiz to find out.

1. You would opt to watch television instead of taking a drive in the country.   T/F

2. When you take a holiday, you prefer to stay in a five-star resort.   T/F

3. A fantasy holiday might include a trip to a nature reserve in Africa.   T/F

4. You believe that natural elements like water, fire, air and other natural properties are here solely to serve humans.   T/F

5. When you feel stressed and upset, you find relief by going outside.   T/F

6. You recall at least one moment where you felt in awe of nature's power or beauty.   T/F

7. Your favourite place in the world includes a natural element.   T/F

8. You enjoy the changing seasons and weather.   T/F

9. You feel a deep connection with animals.   T/F

10. You'd rather eradicate spiders than notice their webs.   T/F

What did you discover?

If you find yourself focused more on materialism than Mother Nature, and answered 'true' to questions 1, 2, 4 and 10, you may want to re-evaluate your relationship with the natural world and find a way to restore it as part of your own self-actualization.

How nature deepens spirituality

No matter how disciplined your practice or how often you seek the silence needed to hear your soul speak, there will be moments when doubt sneaks in and challenges your faith. This is why spirituality must be consistently practised and encouraged. Sacred spaces must be sought out and revered. In no place is it easier to restore faith than when surrounded by the mysteries and marvels of the natural world. In fact, when we are disconnected from our environment, we are missing out on a chance to connect deeply with our own nature.

It's no coincidence that, as we've moved into the cities and become consumers rather than foragers and hunters, we've also grown more unconscious of and disconnected from our own spirituality. Because the natural environment is one aspect of our awakening, we remain off balance and out of touch when we don't have a connection to it.

Key idea

When we are disconnected from our natural environment, we are also disconnected from our own true nature. We are of the natural world, and only when we nourish our relationship with it can we be in harmony with higher consciousness.

The natural spaces in our world offer clear, tangible examples of the universe at work. We don't have to understand how all that creation works to know that it is always expanding and growing in perfect harmony.

There is much we don't know about Mother Nature; many mysteries of Gaia are still unexplored. We are unable to harness the hurricanes or to manage the tides, yet we see them shape our land and our lives. We still do not know with any certainty whether life exists on other planets and we don't know unequivocally how the solar system evolved. And yet we have faith. We have faith that the sun we see will rise each day, giving birth to new life. We know the mountains will persist long after our buildings fall into rubble, and spiders will continue to create intricate webs around nothing more than a blade of grass.

Remember this

The way to spiritual balance and awakening can be found, in part, by appreciating the natural world to which we all belong. Seek out information about nature to remind yourself how amazing our ecosystem is. Continue to study and marvel at the complexity and perfection of our environment. It is amazing, for example, that the tip of an elephant's trunk is so sensitive and flexible that it can pick up a pin.

Try it now

Get up and look out of the window. Allow your eye to be drawn to a flower or blade of grass or another growing thing. As you look at this living thing, consider these questions and answer them in your journal: 'How are we connected?' 'How can we sustain each other?'

Nature works perfectly, without our meddling and without our management: *that* we can have faith in. When we allow nature to be, and watch it unfold with respect, reverence and wonder, we also become conscious and aware of our own true nature – one that is just as beautiful, powerful and miraculous as the one we witness in our external environment. When we understand, appreciate and experience our natural world, we know ourselves better and we recognize that we are all part of the same creative force. We see that we, too, are an expression of nature.

GUIDED BY THE GODDESS MOTHER EARTH

For centuries, indigenous people lived in harmony with the land. The Pawnee, a native American tribe, worshipped Atira, goddess of the earth and the sacred mother of every living creature. She was treated with great respect.

Numerous other tribes and aboriginal populations prayed to Mother Earth. Their mythology often took on characteristics of wild animals; they farmed and hunted as needed, demonstrating gratitude and wonder for the gifts of the landscape.

> 'The Indian made an effort to know of spiritual things from his own observations of nature, because all truth can be found in nature. There is a spiritual beauty in the realization that the world has been deliberately made or created, and is in perfect balance ecologically, and that is not by chance.'
>
> Eli Gatoga, Cherokee (1914–83)

Paganism is another tradition rooted in a reverence for nature. Mother Earth is an aspect of God, according to pagan beliefs. In this way, your spirit is not separate from the snowflakes or the river current. Everything is connected. When you work for the protection and preservation of the natural environment, you also begin to heal parts of yourself.

HUMANS: PART OF NATURE, NOT SUPERIOR TO IT

As humans have acquired awareness and knowledge of their environment, they have constantly sought to rein in and control the natural world. We have raged against the forces of nature, cursed her storms, floods and earthquakes. We have tried to control Mother Nature by trapping her behind our dams and sea-walls, within our pipelines and under our concrete. In the process, we've eliminated acres of sacred spaces and obliterated any balance that existed between our natural world and our humanity.

However, as Father Richard Rohr says, nature isn't something we can ultimately fix, control or forever change. Instead, it is we who must adapt. Until we do, until we live in harmony with all creatures, until we look on the natural elements with awe and respect and appreciation and sacredness, our separation from higher consciousness will continue.

Try it now

We rely on nature for so much. Today, it's time to give back. Do one thing today that celebrates your relationship with the outdoors. Maybe you take a walk outside instead of driving to the gym. Perhaps you begin composting. Maybe you plant a garden, or shop at an outdoor market. Take compassionate action in appreciation of the natural world. Think of it as a gift, one that will support your partnership with the planet.

Nature is not something to be channelled or belittled. It is not an inferior dimension, to be controlled, managed or used into extinction. Nor is it an insignificant piece of our spiritual experience. Instead, to connect with nature is to connect to our higher consciousness. Should we choose to nurture that, to know it, to harmonize with it, we step into the realm of conscious creation.

Remember this

We are an integral part of an entire system, no better or worse than any other element on the planet. Our place is as a part of it all, not separate from it. When we awaken to this understanding, we awaken to our spirit.

Key idea

'The human being is a social animal. I often tell my friends that they have no need to study philosophy, these professional, complicated subjects. By simply looking at these innocent animals, insects, ants, bees, etc., quite often I develop some kind of respect for them. How? Because they have no religion, no constitution, no police force, nothing. But they live in harmony through the natural law of existence or nature's law or system.'

His Holiness the 14th Dalai Lama of Tibet

The practice of ecopsychology

The dependence of our physical, psychological and spiritual wellbeing on a compassionate connection to nature is driving the emergence of a new therapeutic model called ecopsychology.

Ecopsychologists believe that we cannot be completely healthy or whole as long as we are isolated from our environment. A lifestyle that promotes harmony between people and nature will benefit not only our physical and mental health but also our relationships and our own personal and spiritual growth. It will also ease the guilt and sadness many people feel about not doing enough to sustain the environment.

Many families experience depression, anxiety and despair when they consider the large-scale environmental problems that exist and see how little they are doing, or are able to do, to make a difference, says psychologist and teacher Thomas Joseph Doherty. These negative emotions can actually help us become more aware of our innate need for natural connection. When we recognize that we feel better when we nurture our relationship with the environment, we are more likely to protect it, cultivate it, nourish it and be nourished by it.

Often, though, we don't recognize our need for a nature intervention – until we get sick, feel overwhelmed, off balance or depressed. Then we know intuitively that we need to get close to Mother Earth. We escape to the beaches or the seclusion and tranquillity of the mountains. We immerse ourselves in natural hot springs or go for long walks. We turn the soil under our fingertips. We bring fresh flowers into the house. And we feel better.

Remember this

Next time you're feeling stressed or upset, get outside. Immerse yourself in the beauty of nature. Feel the dirt on your fingertips or listen to the sound of water gurgling in the stream. When we feel off balance, it's because we are cut off from a piece of our spirit. Nature is one way to reconnect.

THE HEALING POWER OF NATURE

Nature's healing power is due in part to the way we're wired. Environmental elements produce specific physiological responses. For example, we relax when we're surrounded by lush, vegetative environments. We are attracted to and moved by natural beauty.

Some scientists explain this response through the biophilia hypothesis, which says that our genes have evolved to produce good feelings whenever we're surrounded by healthy, vital, lush environments. In this way, our ancient ancestors were naturally drawn to environments that were rich in life-sustaining elements like an abundance of food, safe water supplies and natural shelter.

Today, most of our basic needs are met in other ways. Few of us hunt for food or have to seek out fresh water. But our spiritual survival still depends on the environment.

Key idea

We are hardwired to care for and connect to the environment. Physically, it supports our bodies and biological systems and helps us to heal. Spiritually, it supports us through connection, awe, and harmony. To be a healthy physical and spiritual being is to be in harmony with the natural world.

Hundreds of studies list the benefits of fostering this connection with nature. Exposure to the natural environment helps to:

- improve patient healing after surgery
- reduce stress
- lower blood pressure and heart rate
- reduce fear
- minimize aggressive behaviour.

In one study from Texas A&M University, patients who were able to look at natural scenery outside their hospital window required less pain medication than those who weren't. In another, published in the *Journal of the Japanese Institute of Landscape Architecture,* study participants who looked at a green hedge felt relaxed, while those who stared at a concrete wall actually experienced a sharp increase in stress.

The relationship between the natural environment and our health and wellbeing is so critical that hospitals are now designing therapeutic gardens in their grounds and even remodelling care facilities themselves to incorporate waterfalls, water features and gardens. These days, lobbies are filled with indoor plants and landscape photographs, and wards are constructed with more windows.

Sunlight is also a powerful healer. Natural light can ease depression and shorten hospital stays. Even photographs of natural scenes are effective in reducing pain and anxiety.

Case study: Rob

It was while visiting his father's native country, India, that Rob, a software engineer, began exploring his own spirituality. Now Rob says his spiritual connection is nourished by nature. Being outdoors, he says, helps him balance the intrusion and noise of the built-up world with his own self-awareness. While he sees the value of mass media, the Internet and social connections, it can be hard to shut it all out to hear spirit speak. So, he finds quiet by getting away from it all.

'Most of my spiritual practices are nature based: watching a sunset or sitting in a quiet garden, or primitive camping away from most [people and things],' says Rob. 'I don't have a regular practice, but when I'm in solitude or nature, I find that there is an immense amount of clarity I can gain. Nature is the link to our truth – the eternal,' he says. 'Nature-wise, only the grass and the truth will prevail.'

When he's facing a challenge in life or working to understand relationships, Rob also uses meditation to discover insight and understanding.

'If I'm faced with a difficult decision, I find that meditation helps me form my answers. It's not always easy, nor does it always occur in 30 minutes. In some cases, I've found it takes months of disjointed meditation and reflection to understand the correct answers.' But meditation and the faith he has in something bigger than himself have helped him through sleepless nights when he'd felt as though he had no one to talk to.

'Truthfully, I sometimes meditate in bed, comfortably, just before going to sleep. I try to fill my head with good thoughts, which lead to sweet dreams.'

Try it now

Make time this week to bring the outdoors in. Choose a beautiful flower or plant and put it in the indoor space that you spend the most time in. Perhaps you're drawn to crystals or a desktop water feature. Find a natural element that attracts you and set it in a visible place. Then, each day, develop a ritual around recognizing and appreciating this item that is now sharing your space.

THE IMPORTANCE OF CONSCIOUS CONNECTION

If you stray too far from the natural world, the chances are you will also lose sight of your interdependence on nature. Without that connection, it's easier to feel separate and superior to the environment. This is a dangerous position to take, because it fuels ego-based actions rather than choices that nurture both the environment and the people within it.

When we are operating from ego and focused only on our individual power, we tend to consider our own desires, comforts and needs before we look at them in relation to the planet. For example, we look at bottom-line profits before considering the pollution levels caused by factory production. We think of the comfort and ease of travelling by car before we worry about oil refineries. We decide it's easier for us to throw things away instead of recycling.

We become unconscious in our actions and inadvertently contribute to the destruction of the natural world. In the process, we also lose a bit of our own inner landscape without ever realizing it.

THE POWER OF RECONNECTION

A reconnection to the planet revs up our compassion and appreciation. When we hear the roar of the ocean or feel the grass under our bare feet, when we notice the osprey sitting atop an ancient fir or a bee collecting pollen from a flower, we feel part of something bigger. This sense of unity piques our awareness. We become mindful of the tendrils of life extending throughout the universe.

Instead of being so self-absorbed, reactive and unaware, we tend to be more benevolent. We become more patient and curious. When we know, in a deep way, that we are part of the whole, a natural part of the evolving universe, we become more compassionate towards all living things. In this way, we begin to heal ourselves and breach the separation from our souls.

Remember this

In order to restore peace, health and harmony to our lives and expand into higher consciousness, we must consciously immerse ourselves in nature. Schedule time for this each week. Plan for it and make it happen. Watch a sunset, eat lunch on a park bench, or plan a trip to the coast and watch the waves roll in. You'll feel the health benefits within minutes and your spirit will rejoice.

Try it now

Take off your shoes and leave them off as you walk through the world during the next hour. Notice the smooth coolness of wood floors under your feet and give silent thanks for the trees that grew to provide them, or feel the fibres of a carpet and recognize the source of wool or the natural resources it took for it to be created. Go outside and feel the rough cobblestones or the grass of a lawn. For so long, we have been removed from the environment. It is essential that you allow it back in.

How to restore your relationship with the natural world

▶ Become mindful of what is already around you.

Even in a built environment, there are plenty of opportunities to connect with nature. Become aware of all that surrounds you and go looking for natural elements. Notice the clouds above or a ladybird on the shrub outside. Appreciate the dandelion pushing through the cracks in the pavement. Become aware of the integration between our natural selves and the natural world.

▶ Go outside.

Each day, make a point to be out in the air. Breathe it in. Feel the rain or splash through the puddles. Go for a walk on your lunch break. Watch the clouds. Ten minutes outside will ease your stress and remind you of your connection to the bigger forces.

▶ Bring the outside in.

Greenery in your office helps foster creativity and ease anxiety. When we surround ourselves with the marvels of nature, we are reminded of its beauty and importance. Bring in fresh flowers and mindfully arrange them in a vase. Cultivate seedlings in pots on your windowsill until they are ready to be planted outside. Display crystals, known for their powerful energies, on your windowsill. Pause throughout the day to appreciate these elements.

▶ Look out of the window.

Take two minutes to gaze out of the window at different times during your day. Each time, challenge yourself to notice different aspects of the natural world. See how the sun shifts. Notice the different cloud formations or the pattern of the blowing leaves. Even in the middle of our biggest cities, nature will prevail. Life feels marvellously optimistic when we notice it.

▶ Create a relationship with one natural element.

Some ecopsychologists suggest that people establish a relationship with a single object in their regular environment and foster that relationship. Start by going outside and becoming mindful to what's around. Notice what you're drawn to. Where is the energy coming from? Many believe that the natural world 'speaks to us' and, if we notice, we can connect with it deeply. But, like any relationship, the one with nature must be respected and nurtured. If you feel a bond with a special tree in your garden, show it some attention every day.

▶ Nurture your pet or any living creatures that cross your path.

Take a moment each day to really connect with the animals that come into your life. Instead of distractedly petting them while doing something else, make time to stop and focus on giving them some love.

▶ **Choose outdoor activities.**

Our disconnection from the environment often begins when we create routines that rely on our built-up infrastructure. Next time you're going to exercise, choose to go for a walk out of doors rather than hitting the treadmill at the gym. When you can, purchase your food at an open-air farmers' market. Eat outdoors. Cycle instead of driving. Look for one way each day to get out of doors.

▶ **Get wet.**

Water – the sound, feel and hydrating qualities of it – are literally life giving. Don't simply drink it down or take a quick shower or swim without affirming its natural powers and essential energies. Appreciating your connection to water and recognizing that it is a basic component of life for all on this planet – including you – is a reminder of the relationship between humans and nature.

Dr Masaru Emoto has studied the molecular structure of water for decades and has photographed water crystals changing in response to negative and positive energies. When we act or speak with words of gratitude and love, water molecules develop beautiful crystals. When water molecules are exposed to words of hate, anger and hostility, they are severely deformed.

Whenever you spend time alongside a beautiful river, immerse yourself in a hot bath or sip a cool drink, take a minute to give thanks to the water and all the natural elements that are available to support and sustain your body and your spirit.

Remember this

The next time you take a drink of water, pause and give genuine thanks for this life-sustaining substance. The more often we recognize how interrelated we are to the natural environment, the more powerful our connection becomes.

Key idea

One way to restore your relationship with the natural world is to invite it into your life. Touch it, smell it, notice it and interact with it whenever you get the chance – even if it's simply while walking to the car. Compassionately and mindfully interact with it each day. Don't be held captive in buildings and stations and cars and shops. Find ways to co-operate with nature, even while doing routine things like shopping or commuting.

Focus points

* To grow spiritually, we must reconnect and restore our relationship with the natural world. We, too, are an essential part of this world, not something separate from or superior to it.
* When we are disconnected from the natural environment, we tend to feel off balance and unhealthy.
* The emerging practice of ecopsychology promotes harmony between people and nature as a way of healing.
* When we become mindful of and compassionate to the natural elements that appear in our daily life, we begin to integrate our spiritual side with our life experience.
* One way to restore our relationship with nature is to interact physically with it by bringing plants, crystals and other elements indoors and by making time each day to get outside and notice the marvels around us.

Next step

When we spiritually connect to the natural environment, we move into relationship with it. This interdependence promotes compassion and kindness, expanding our spiritual awareness beyond knowledge of God and into unity with God. Love and compassion are the highest expressions of self, awakening us to who we are. The next chapter explores compassion and the power of giving and gratitude.

11

Living a life of compassionate service

In this chapter you will learn:

- ► *what compassion is and how to apply it to yourself and others*
- ► *how good feelings spread*
- ► *the importance of serving others*
- ► *five practical ways to serve others*
- ► *why receiving is as important as giving*
- ► *how to establish a practice of gratitude.*

Self-assessment: How compassionate are you?

Is compassion working in your life? Take this quiz to find out.

1 When someone is experiencing a difficult time, what do you do?

   a Offer them support and kindness

   b Feel their pain and have a hard time doing anything but worry

   c Tell them to stop whining because everyone has problems

2 What do you do when you make a mistake?

   a Feel frustrated, but recognize that errors are part of being human

   b Try to cover it up so that no one else discovers the error

   c Ignore it

3 When you're feeling bad, what do you do?

   a Try to help others instead of worrying about your own stuff

   b Complain and whine to anyone who will listen

   c Go shopping or watch television

4 When is compassion a good quality to draw on?

   a Any time

   b When someone is deserving of kindness

   c When you want something

5 When you act with compassion, what are you doing?

   a Offering kindness to yourself and others

   b Donating money to charitable organizations

   c Unaware of what you are doing

6 What do you think when you are kind to someone else?

   a They are more likely to be kind to others

   b They are lucky that you are such a nice person

   c It's not a big deal either way

7 What changes when you act compassionately?

  a Your blood pressure lowers and you feel better

  b Everyone else feels good, but your feelings aren't impacted

  c Nothing changes

8 What is the practice of gratitude?

  a Appreciation

  b Noticing what you like

  c A New Age trend with little benefit

9 Graciously receiving a compliment or gift from another is what?

  a An important part of compassion and gratitude

  b Embarrassing and uncomfortable

  c Not a big deal

10 What is serving others?

  a An uplifting aspect of spiritual awakening

  b A way to stop feeling sorry for yourself

  c Hard to do when you've got so much to deal with in your own life

What did you discover?

If you circled mostly **a** answers, you are already benefiting from the power of gratitude and compassion. These two qualities supercharge your spiritual experience by helping you to connect positively and powerfully with yourself and others. If you circled mostly **b**s and **c**s, you may feel unhappy or unfulfilled. Try giving back to someone else and your own mood will soar.

Living with compassion

One of the surest circuits to spirit is compassion. Compassion, empathy, kindness, benevolent love or showing concern for the health and wellbeing of others is the road on which spirit travels. When we live with compassion, we directly experience the divine and we are able to connect with ourselves and others in a deep and authentic way. We are living from the highest energies of the universe and awakening to our essence.

Key idea

When we are acting with compassion, we are having a direct experience of the divine. We are one with higher consciousness and operating from love, the highest energy of the universe.

Of course, compassion can enrich your daily life beyond measure. There is great joy when we can give to others. There is great peace when we can offer our kindness. And this kind of unselfish love can literally change the world.

The look of compassion

A friend loses a loved one, so you send flowers. Another is ill with cancer, so you take meals to her family so that she doesn't have to cook. One fails to get on to the Masters course he applied for, and you reach out with support and solace to help him cope with the disappointment. You volunteer to care for animals at the pet shelter. You forgive yourself for a mistake.

These are all acts of compassion. They are decidedly practical, yet they elevate human interaction into an expression of love that unites us with the highest energy of the universe.

When we reach out to ease the pain of someone who is hurting, we are acting compassionately. When we do something with no thought of repayment – but only to uplift, improve, love or make another positive contribution – we are acting compassionately. It's a natural expression of who we are. We are wired for this.

Relating to others and helping them in a loving way are part of our essence, but this essence at times is stifled by ego. Our ego tells us that we've got to look out for ourselves to be a success in this world, but the reality is that, when we act compassionately toward others, we benefit in a big way. It is a form of self-care. Compassion is one thing that is good for everyone.

Remember this

Next time you're with a friend in trouble and you aren't sure what to do, just listen. Don't interrupt. Don't offer advice. Just look them in the eye and be present with them by nodding your head and acknowledging their words. Sometimes all we need is to be heard, and compassion can validate the experience and help us feel less alone. It's a gift to be able to be with someone in their pain without trying to change it.

HOW SELF-COMPASSION WORKS

Self-compassion is the act of being kind to yourself even when you've been less than perfect. It's about extending patience and kindness even when you're in emotional or physical pain. It is not an excuse to go soft. Self-compassion requires you to see the experience for what it is, to be accountable to it, but then it allows you to respond with love and support rather than anger or criticism.

Perhaps this seems a little self-indulgent or selfish. We are raised with the paradoxical belief that we should first do for others before we do for ourselves. We are taught not to rely on others for anything. In fact, you may even think that you are not worthy of compassion.

On the contrary, by treating yourself to a little compassion, you will become more productive, more accountable and more self-aware. It is a healthier way of dealing with adversity and error. If we are kind to ourselves, we don't need to hide from the truth. We are no longer afraid of it. We can stand in all of it, see the situation for what it is, and accept responsibility.

Then we learn how to do better next time. This is a motivating, productive way to live. Instead of denying or resisting, we are accepting our circumstances and responding in an active way.

When we stay rooted in self-criticism or anger, we tend to be less motivated to do anything. Not only are we unable to help ourselves, but we also have less to offer others. When we are kind to ourselves, we are less stressed and more open. From that positive place, we have more to offer others.

Try it now

Think of a mistake you've made, a time when you really blew it. Write it down in a sentence or two on a piece of paper. Then crumple up the paper and throw it away or burn it. As you do this, release the angst over the error and replace it with compassion, understanding and maybe even a laugh. Recognize your humanity, the one that is prone to mistakes once in a while. When you can live in those difficult moments with compassion for yourself, you will also be more likely to offer compassion to others.

Remember this

If you want to make improvements in your life, self-compassion can help. It allows you to see your error, respond with kindness and make adjustments to keep it from happening again. Self-criticism often keeps us locked in fear and unwilling to try again.

CHOOSING COMPASSION

You can choose to act compassionately. You can choose to reach out with kindness – or not. This is a decision you make. It is not one that depends on the behaviour of others or how well your day is going. There are no conditions that must be met before you can act with compassion. There is nothing anyone has to do to deserve it. Compassion does not need to be earned. If you're dedicated to living a spiritual life, if you want to awaken to the universal source, you will live with compassion and love. There is no other way.

Compassion doesn't mean you take over or try to shield others from pain or difficulty. You simply share it with them. You love them, offering patience and support. You act out of concern for others and, as that act of love infuses them, you may be surprised at how it uplifts you.

Key idea

Compassion does not have to be earned. It is not a reward you dole out. It is a choice you make – in your own life – whether to act compassionately from spirit or not. Everyone is worthy – even if they make you mad or upset – it is up to you to decide whether you will respond with kindness or criticism.

The benefits of compassionate living

Acts of compassion or altruism – defined by some researchers as 'unselfish, benevolent love' – reduce our stress response. Compassionate or altruistic acts like volunteering have been shown to boost immune function, ease pain and contribute to lingering feelings of happiness for both the giver and receiver.

Try it now

Right now, send an email or handwritten note to someone you care about. Before you start writing, take a moment to consider the qualities you appreciate in them. Then, write the note mentioning at least one of those qualities. Send it, and take a minute to reflect on the good feelings that the recipient will experience when they receive your note. Notice your feelings, too, and write in your journal about the entire experience. When we are tuned into our own compassion, we are usually less judgmental and more able to identify additional ways to help others.

Altruistic behaviour may also lengthen our lives, according to evolutionary psychologist Stephanie Brown. Brown studied 423 couples for five years and found that those who helped others were likely to live longer than those who gave no support.

Those who offer physical and emotional support to others also experience greater, lingering happiness; researchers have dubbed this phenomenon the 'helper's high'. The helper's high is described as the warm, pleasant feelings that come after helping another person. Many of those feelings can be resurrected long after the compassionate act is over. Simply remembering the good deed causes people to feel good all over again.

The physiological responses to compassionate behaviour are so strong that people not only feel more energized after helping out but find that their responses counteract the effects of stress, according to Dr Kathleen Hall, founder of The Stress Institute. While we are acting with compassion to ease the pain of others, we are feeling better ourselves and that motivates us to do more. Such is the cycle of love. What you give out comes back to you.

Remember this

If you're mired in the mess of your own life and feeling low, find a way to reach out to someone else. Mow your neighbour's lawn, let a stranger jump the queue in front of you, drop off a dinner for a friend and imagine how good that will make them feel. The fastest way to better feelings is to do something for someone else.

THE SPREAD OF GOOD FEELINGS

In a very tangible way, then, these good feelings pass from one person to another through a process that psychologists call 'emotional contagion'. When you're feeling good, you're infecting others with those good feelings. When you're expressing anger or frustration, you're bringing down the moods of the others around you.

When you reach out with compassion, love and kindness, not only do you experience the positive physiological boost that comes from sharing love, but the recipient is also receiving much-needed support and the positive energy from your good mood. They then feel better, and those who come into contact with those people pick up on their positive vibes and feel better too. In a very real way, we can 'infect' the entire world with compassion and kindness.

LIVING A LIFE OF SERVICE

A sure way to keep this cycle of compassion going is to live a life of service. This doesn't require you to give away all your income or volunteer all your time. Living a service-oriented life does, however, require you to raise your level of awareness so that you can adequately identify the needs of others and then respond in a selfless way.

Living just one day of a service-oriented life may call on you to hold the hand of a friend in hospital, or listen to your mother share her concerns about ageing, or offer a smile and a thank you to a stressed-out bus driver. There are scores of ways to uplift others. When you are paying attention and living with a genuine desire to serve, you will know just how to help.

> **Key idea**
>
> Acts of compassion don't have to be big to make a big difference in the world.

Five ways to serve others

We may feel as though we must commit a lot of time and resources to make a big difference, but this is not so. It's often the little things that change someone's day or leave them (and you) feeling uplifted.

Here are five surprising ways to make a difference in the world.

▶ Send a note telling someone you love how much they mean to you.

▶ Offer a genuine smile to the bank tellers, bus drivers and others who help you each day.

▶ Listen without interruption to anyone who needs to talk.

▶ Raise a compassionate and kind child.

▶ Volunteer for the jobs no one else wants to do.

COMPASSION STARTS WITH CURIOSITY AND AWARENESS

When you live a life of service, you are committed to connecting with people where they are, in the moment, and responding in a way that is kind, loving and helpful. This takes some curiosity and awareness. You must be genuinely interested in the people with whom you come into contact in order to understand their unique struggle and experience. Then you can approach them from a place of empathy.

You don't have to share their struggle, or even have experienced it yourself to understand their pain. Pain is universal. You don't need to have an opinion or any advice to offer. You don't need to weigh in on their experience at all. Rather than judging them, awareness allows you to empathize with them and reach out in a supportive and appropriate manner.

This doesn't always feel good. Sometimes it may seem easier to withhold your kindness or to act out in anger, particularly when someone has lashed out at you. You may feel it is easier to judge those who are repeating the mistakes that lead to so much pain rather than offer them your empathy.

But all people need a daily dose of compassion, and those who behave in a way that is difficult to deal with or understand are often the ones who need our compassion the most. They are starved of kindness. In a moment, you can deliver a dose of love or connection that can ease their pain – and yours.

To remain in judgment or anger is to stifle your spiritual side and will only cause you – and others – more pain and stress. Compassion is the way out. It is freeing. When we are committed to living a life of service, it isn't our job to judge. It is our job *only* to love. We can do that any time, anywhere.

Receiving is as important as giving

Part of living a compassionate life is to be receptive to gifts from others. When you receive their kindness, their gifts, their compliments or their verbal support, you are allowing them to live out their purpose of compassion. Don't turn away from the kindnesses bestowed upon you. Be gracious. Welcome in the gifts and attention. Offer sincere thanks and allow yourself time to experience the love that they are offering you. Not only will you feel good, but you will be giving them a gift too – by allowing them to reap the rewards of their compassionate act.

Key idea

When people are lashing out in anger or repeatedly making bad choices, they are likely to be suffering from compassion deficit. And when they act badly, it's our tendency to respond, in our frustration, with anger or judgment. By choosing a life of compassionate service, you decide to do it differently. You choose to meet everyone and everything with compassion and kindness. When you can do that, you have a real chance of changing the world.

Remember this

It is as important to receive as it is to give. When someone offers you a gift or compliment, don't dismiss it. Receive the gift and offer a genuine thank you. By being gracious you are giving a gift in return.

Try it now

Write down three things you can do to help others today, and make it happen. After completing each act, write about what you did in your journal, and then describe how you felt before and after the act.

GRATITUDE POWERS UP COMPASSION

One of the benefits of living with greater compassion is that it helps you become aware of all that is working in your life. Often, when we step towards the suffering of others, we see our own lives in new ways. For example, you may not fully appreciate your job until your friend loses his. When you can be compassionate and present to the lives of others, you are more likely to be grateful for all that you have.

Gratitude is therefore one of the most practical, in-the-moment exercises available to connect you with source energy and self. It can immediately transform your life into a spiritual exploration.

What is gratitude?

Gratitude is a present-moment practice that helps you recognize both the major and the minor blessings that surround you in every phase of life. It requires that you notice the goodness that often gets overlooked, and it requires you actively to give and appreciate these things.

When you participate in a gratitude practice, your consciousness shifts and so does your life experience. Suddenly your life is filled with good things and alive with moments to be thankful for – even in troubling times.

It's similar to buying, say, a new car. You never paid much attention to the cars on the road until you bought, for example, a new Volkswagen. Then you see Volkswagens everywhere. It's not that the entire world has bought new VWs at the same time; it's only that you're noticing them for the first time. Similarly, with gratitude: when you begin searching for the good things going on, they start appearing everywhere.

When you become clear about what is working in your life, you become braver and more resilient. You are less resistant to change, less fearful of uncertainty and more likely to act compassionately and kindly towards others. It's win–win.

HOW GRATITUDE WORKS

In order to become grateful, we must pause and become aware of what is. Then, instead of focusing on all that is hard or painful in our struggle, gratitude shifts our focus to all that is right. This can transform our experience from bad to good, because energy flows to what we focus on. When we're focused on positives, we experience more to feel positive about.

Key idea

Gratitude is a practice that brings you into the present moment and helps you become aware of all the goodness in your life. When you pause to appreciate things that you might otherwise overlook, you feel happier, more resilient, more courageous and more connected to the higher power of the universe.

Case study: Heather

For Heather, the day begins with a spiritual writing practice. Each morning, she releases her resentments and fears on paper, explores other issues and concerns, and then writes about gratitude.

She started her gratitude practice about six years ago because she realized she was focusing primarily on the negative things in her life – always expecting the worst – and missing out on the good things altogether.

'I had to practise retraining my brain to notice the big and little things that were gifts,' says Heather. Usually, during her morning writing session, she'll list 10 to 15 things that she's thankful for, ranging from gratitude for her creativity to gratitude for someone giving her a ride home the night before. Recently, she's also done the exercise on Facebook, 'as a way to curb my impulse to complain or feel sorry for myself'. The practice has changed the way she responds to external influences, especially when things go wrong.

'I find I appreciate people, myself and my circumstances more. I feel more joy and I think it's also catching on. People don't actually want to feel bad, they just don't know how to feel good.'

Another aspect of Heather's practice is a God dialogue. She writes a letter to her non-denominational God describing her pain and suffering and then she listens for an answer or insight. Usually, what she hears is reassurance that the pain is a part of life, not a punishment.

'Often, it has literally been just to feel held while I cry. It allows me not to be crippled with fear during times of intense transition. I can get up and do the next thing even if I don't know how it will turn out.' Spirituality has helped Heather let go of things she can't control and helps her feel good.

'It makes me a more positive person because I trust that there is a God who loves me … and who is guiding me. I guess the way I think about it is practical. If believing in a being greater than myself makes me happier and less anxious, which it does, then I'm not going to read too much into it. It makes me feel like I belong and I am loved, and that is priceless.'

In this way, gratitude can help us transcend a limited human experience into an expansive, spiritual one. With gratitude, our awareness grows and, in a very real way, we awaken to both an inner and an outer world that is love-filled and good.

Most of us, though, aren't prone to practise gratitude. We are more likely to ruminate and worry, complain and consider the failings in our lives: all that we lack. Gratitude doesn't work this way. It is not a comparison or conditional. You don't give thanks for something and then disparage it by implying you'd be even more thankful if you had more of it. Gratitude requires you to become aware of what is, and consciously to give thanks for those things that are meaningful to you.

Try it now

At least five times today – seriously, do this five times – acknowledge someone who has helped you, look them in the eye and say 'Thank you'. This acknowledgment is both a demonstration of giving – you are giving them your attention and gratitude – and an aspect of receiving, because you took time to appreciate the help they offered you.

It takes both giving and receiving to live a life of compassionate service.

Remember this

If you feel as though you have nothing to be grateful for, you aren't paying attention. You don't need big-ticket items like perfect health or a million dollars to ramp up the gratitude machine. Start with what you can see or experience right now, in the moment. If you have a hand to hold this book, or eyes with which you are able to read it, you have plenty to be grateful for. A gratitude practice isn't about creating new experiences to appreciate; it's about deeply appreciating all that you already have.

Try it now

Stop what you're doing right now and jot down three things that you're grateful for. Be specific. When you pause briefly to notice what is working in your life, you'll see the good things everywhere.

THREE STEPS TO ESTABLISHING GRATITUDE PRACTICE

It's easy to establish gratitude practice, and it's a powerful way to start and end the day. Take the following steps, and then make a commitment to start a daily practice.

1 **Take a break and breathe.** Pause, and inhale deeply three times. Feel your body relax and become present to all that is in the moment.

2 **Acknowledge what is working well.** Notice the people or things or gifts you received that were meaningful or important. Pay attention to the important lessons learned or pivotal life experiences.

3 **Give thanks.** Pick one or several of these things and say 'Thank you' aloud, or jot it down in your journal. Choose several things each day to be grateful for.

TIPS TO HELP YOUR PRACTICE

▶ **Be specific.** Don't just say that you're thankful for your good health; give thanks for your healthy heart, low blood pressure or good eyesight.

▶ **Infuse each item with emotion.** Pause after declaring what you're grateful for and experience the emotion that comes. If you're grateful for a payment you received today, feel the emotion of relief that comes, along with knowing that you can now cover your costs or build your savings. If you're giving thanks to your spouse for cooking dinner, experience the feelings of love and comfort that you felt when you sat down to the meal.

▶ **Challenge yourself to find new things.** Don't repeat things on your gratitude list from day to day. Look for new treasures to be grateful for. Soon, you'll find yourself appreciating things all day long, simply so that you can add them to your list.

▶ **Consider things both big and small.** How do you measure the importance of one breath against another? They are both equally significant. The same is true for the items you choose to be grateful for. Gratitude is simply a conscious practice of appreciation and there is much to appreciate – even on the hard days. The so-called little things – watching the sunrise, feeling the breath in your lungs or enjoying a drink of water – matter. Everything matters. Nothing is too small.

► **Mix it up.** In the morning, it may work to give thanks aloud for three things as you start your day. In the evening, you may prefer to keep a written gratitude list in your journal and then write more about each item as you reflect on your day. There is no wrong way to keep up your practice. Just make sure you do it daily.

Focus points

✲ Compassion – acting with unselfish love and concern for another – is a way of expressing love and the highest expression of ourselves.

✲ Because we are all connected and everything is interrelated, when we act compassionately, we also experience profound benefits such as better health and happiness.

✲ Compassion is a choice. You decide whether to live compassionately – or not. Nobody has to earn it. Everyone is worthy. The most belligerent or angry people are often functioning from a compassion deficit.

✲ Serving others is one way to live a healthier life and uplift the world because the good feelings that emerge from kindness spread to others.

✲ Gratitude is one way to boost compassion. To be grateful, you must become aware of what's good in your life. When you do that, you are more likely to reach out and share those good feelings with others.

Next step

To live a compassionate life, we must become aware of what others are experiencing and offer them our love and support. When we can do this, we are aligned with our higher self. This is the route to truth and authenticity. The next chapter explains how to live an authentic life and thereby thrive and live your purpose.

12

Stepping into your authenticity

In this chapter you will learn:

- ▶ *what authenticity is*
- ▶ *how it can help you thrive during difficult times*
- ▶ *four ways to access your authenticity*
- ▶ *how to discover your passion and purpose*
- ▶ *tips for living a spiritual life.*

Self-assessment: Are you living an authentic life?

Take this true/false quiz to find out.

1 I often feel jealous or insecure.   T/F

2 I am living my life's purpose.   T/F

3 I have a hard time trusting my instincts.   T/F

4 I practise living in the moment.   T/F

5 I have a difficult time making decisions.   T/F

6 I find meaning even in the difficult times.   T/F

7 I'd rather not look at my faults and imperfections.   T/F

8 I know what my faults are and I take responsibility for them.   T/F

9 I experience setbacks as learning opportunities.   T/F

10 I feel engaged and responsive to life rather than reactive.   T/F

What did you discover?

If you answered 'true' to most of the even-numbered questions and number 9, you are living with the kind of self-awareness that breeds authenticity. You feel true to yourself. You know what your values are and you connect with them daily. You're willing to look at and experience your flaws and failings, knowing that they are an aspect of self and a route to knowledge.

If you answered 'true' to the odd-numbered questions and 'false' to the even numbers, you're not quite sure just yet who you are. You often judge yourself based on your public image or external criteria. You may feel as though you don't measure up to the expectations of others and you spend time feeling tight, and nervous that others will discover your flaws and failings.

Who are you?

From the time we have our first glimpse of our self as a separate being, at around the age of two, our self-awareness begins to develop and shape our lives. We become aware of our emotions and our bodies. We begin to consider our roles and responsibilities in our families and communities, and we pay attention to how others see us.

We then might ask the question 'Who am I?' and our search for the answers can define our spiritual life. In many cases, though, we allow the answer to come not from what we know but from what others say about us. We then describe ourselves through societal filters and see ourselves not as we are but as others think we are.

When we're at school, we believe we're clever because the teacher gives us an A. We decide we're unattractive when our first teenage crush doesn't ask us out. We define ourselves as fun and popular when we're invited to a party, and we see ourselves as successful when we get a good job. We are also likely to think we are a failure if we don't get that job or a pay rise, or that we are unworthy of love when someone abuses us.

Our sense of self, then, is largely a reflection of the things outside us. We take those perspectives in, mould our behaviour and ideas around them, shape them into a form that we can live with and adopt this as our 'true self'.

Key idea

While your sense of self is often a reflection of external influences and the thoughts of others, these are never an accurate portrayal of who you really are, authentically. When you live a more spiritual life and become more self-aware, your true self begins to emerge.

When you live authentically, you go inside to your core to consider whether the choices at hand are consistent with your spirit and your value system. This makes decisions easier and you remain accountable to the outcomes. Life opens up for you and you are actively engaged and responding creatively and enthusiastically to whatever appears.

If you are unsure who you really are, you agonize over decisions, worrying that you will make the wrong one and, although you believe you have a greater purpose on earth, you have no clue what that is.

But you will find it. You will know your purpose when you know yourself.

Try it now

Write down all the titles and labels that you live with, such as mother, father, wife, husband, son, daughter, house cleaner, CEO, doctor, administrator, woman, man, tennis player, golfer, reader, cook. Then cross off any that don't truly, deeply, accurately express or reflect all of who you are. Now, write down who you know yourself to be.

When we begin living a more spiritual life, the reflection changes a bit and so does our sense of our self. We begin to question our purpose on this planet, we begin to look deeper for the answer to 'Who am I?' We begin to explore our essence as an extension of spirit and we begin to know ourselves as something bigger than the things we do or the way we look. In other words, we awaken to our authenticity.

Awakening is a product of deep self-awareness – the kind that comes from practice and exploration. And in that process, you begin to know your whole self, the one mixed with imperfections and gifts, the one aligned with spirit and mind and body, the one that is on purpose and true, regardless of external response.

What is authenticity?

Authenticity is a product of who we are within, coupled with how we act. It requires us to use our self-awareness to understand and adapt and stay on course to live consistently from this sense of self.

This means we have to understand our strengths and weaknesses and be honest with ourselves when we make a mistake. We must know our values and live from them. Psychologists Michael Kernis and Brian Goldman say that authenticity requires you to know yourself and then live openly with all that. They define authenticity as 'the unimpeded operation of one's true or core self in one's daily enterprise'.

When you are living authentically, you are living from your core and your actions align with that essence.

Key idea

Authenticity emerges when you are living and acting in accordance with your core self, including your values, priorities, personal truths, purpose and passions. When you are functioning from a place of personal truth, you feel better, even though this requires you to accept your flaws and failings.

LIVING TRUE TO SELF

This is a powerful way to live. It provides clarity when things may seem confusing or muddled. It provides insight when things may otherwise seem unclear. When you're authentic, when you are living truthfully, you're able to thrive through the tough times because you are not impeded by those doubting inner voices or insecurities about your public image.

Most of us want to live from this place of self-knowing. It takes a lot of the pressure off. If we're being real and honest with ourselves first, we don't have to worry about being found out or discovered to be a fraud. We don't have to hide or tweak or manipulate things to support some ideal image that we feel we need to live up to. Instead, we can put our energies into living and playing and learning and growing.

It's no wonder, then, that authentic people report greater vitality, self-esteem, resilience and wellbeing than those who lack authenticity. When you are living from your truth, you're also bound for happier relationships. This makes sense. Don't you enjoy people who have fewer pretensions? Research shows that authentic people are also more likely to complete their goals, experience more intimacy in relationships, and live life creatively.

Try it now

Remember a time when you felt completely happy and energized. Reflect on it for a minute and experience those positive emotions all over again. Now, go inside that moment and discern exactly what it was that made you feel so good.

Usually, we experience positive emotion when we are connecting deeply with another person, when we are in the flow of our passion and purpose or engaged deeply in life. Those things evolve out of authenticity. Trace back the power of your positive feelings and determine whether the good times you remember were tied to the moments when you were most yourself.

Remember this

Next time you catch yourself feeling defensive or making excuses, pause, take a deep breath and consider just what it is that you are defending. When you are acting authentically, there is nothing you need to excuse. When you are choosing actions that are inconsistent with your authentic self, however, you are more likely to feel the need to defend them.

The challenge of authentic living

Though it feels better to live centred in self, it isn't always easy. To live with the truth of who you are, you must look deeply at yourself and recognize all aspects of self – even the things you aren't proud of. You must acknowledge the times when you have made mistakes or been thwarted by ego and irresponsibility. You need to take a clear look at all that you are, including all that psychic garbage that you keep hidden away when guests arrive. Not only do you have to see your imperfections, you've got to let them out, accept them and find meaning in them.

Case study: Jennifer

When her daughter was born disabled and with many health problems, Jennifer began to question everything. No longer connected to the church of her childhood, no longer sure of God or clear about her faith, she began a process of inquiry that led her to greater awareness and authenticity.

'For me, authenticity is about telling the truth, even when it's hard and even when you're getting a lot of pressure to make it pretty,' says Jennifer, 'even when people call you bitter and angry. You know what? Sometimes I am bitter and angry. Sometimes I am also joyful and at peace. All of those are true aspects of me. They're just different parts of me at different times.'

That awareness has led Jennifer to what she calls a spirituality of truth. It challenges her to find the true answers, not just the easy ones, and sometimes that can be a bit uncomfortable.

'I have to check myself every time I'm glib or I start spouting adages ("everything works out for the best!") because, no, actually, it doesn't. I realize I am going for the easy answer instead of the true one. And when I want to censor myself, maybe I'm not ready to talk about that truth, that's okay, but it means I need to sit with it and see why it scares me and understand why I think I can't live that truth.'

It is this kind of self-inquiry and awareness that has helped Jennifer cope with her daughter's ongoing health challenges. It also connects her to others.

'My spirituality is basically about holding other people's hands and saying, "We're in this together." If I don't tell the truth, or if I don't tell the whole truth, I am betraying those people. Yes, it's uncomfortable all the time. It hurts, and I worry that I will come across as a whining victim or a self-indulgent navel-gazer. But when I tell the truth with no other agenda than to tell the truth, I end up doing it right.'

'There isn't [one] right way to do this. You don't have to believe what anyone else believes. Your answers today don't have to be the same as your answers tomorrow. Don't try to be a guru. Just try to be you.'

There is also a real risk that you won't be accepted for who you are. Some people are bound to feel threatened when you don't follow along, play by their rules or put up with certain behaviour. Relationships may change and that can feel frightening and even lonely, for a time.

It's tough, for example, to drop out of medical school to follow your true passion for the arts, when your parents expected you to become a doctor. It's risky to be the whistle-blower when the boss is asking you to violate your personal ethics. It's daunting to come out of the closet and live openly as a homosexual when others may not approve. It's vulnerable to express your true emotions, when others may feel uncomfortable.

These challenges, however, also provide opportunities for growth and self-actualization. They build resilience, confidence, strength and grace. Life takes on greater meaning and peace is possible even with uncertainty. When you're trying to be something that you're not, peace is nearly impossible. You will spend a lot of time feeling insecure, confused, edgy and dissatisfied.

It's worse, then, to live a lie. It's downright interesting and liberating to live truly as yourself.

Remember this

If you realize that you're reverting to unhealthy behaviour such as drinking too much, overeating or surfing the web to excess, take a look at what you're resisting. What is it that you are hiding from or afraid to confront? Write down in your journal what you discover. When we're out of alignment with our authenticity, we unconsciously do things to mask the pain. When you recognize this, you can move back towards your core.

Key idea

At times, it can be a bit difficult to live authentically, particularly when your truth bucks the popular trend or fights against the expectations of others. But know this: to live anything other than your truth is downright debilitating. Once you become aware of all that you are, you must live from that. Then you are an expression of spirit.

Try it now

Think about something that you're doing in your life primarily because others expect it of you. Ask yourself these questions:

▶ Is it congruent with my true self?

▶ Does it meet my value system?

▶ Is it moving me towards my purpose?

▶ Does it inspire or excite me?

If you answer 'no' to any of these questions, take a closer look at this activity or practice and determine whether it's a true expression of who you are or something that is keeping you from being your best, most authentic self.

If you decide that the expectations of others are holding you back from living an authentic life, jot down some notes about what that experience feels like. Write about what you might do, if anything, to change that. There are no wrong answers; this is simply an exercise in awareness. However, when we see the areas where we're living out of alignment from our true nature, we become ready to make a change, no matter how challenging that might be.

Creating an authentic life

Authenticity is completely dependent on self-awareness. To live authentically, you must know what you value, understand what is important, trust your inner source and act in accordance with those truths.

The first step is to get clear and begin that inner exploration. This can be hard to do in the noise of daily life. It requires time in quiet contemplation. It requires you to become present to the moments you are living now and to begin a practice of mindfulness.

By paying attention to your body, environment or breath, you begin to examine yourself and your thoughts in a detached way.

You are open to insight from this state, able to see truth and brave enough to begin the self-inquiry.

This isn't all hard work. It's fascinating to discover what matters to you. It's interesting to understand why you've done some of the things you've done. It is illuminating to see why you've felt unfulfilled even during some of the best times in your life. It's fun to discover new passions and the purpose that is congruent with who you are.

This is how to live a successful, meaningful life. Until you are operating from your core, you won't find even your greatest successes completely satisfying.

Remember this

When you become mindful and present to the moment, stress dissipates and you no longer have to fear what you will find. In this way, with gentle focus on the now, you can examine your greatest needs and biggest fears, your passionate desires and fundamental failings without judgment or retribution. You can notice them, and use the insights gleaned from mindful awareness to shape a more authentic life.

Try it now

Begin to get clear about what is at the foundation of your character. List your top five values and, for each item, write a few sentences describing why it is on the list. Why does it matter? In another sentence, detail how you live that value each day.

If you discover that your actions do not support your values, your life is out of sync with spirit. It's time, then, to backtrack and look for ways to live in alignment with self.

HOW TO ACCESS YOUR AUTHENTICITY

1 Be open to life.

To be authentic is to engage in life: to be open to what comes without excuse or bias, to be present to the moment, and step into the flow of life. In this process you will see, with new clarity, what works for you, and what feels fake or false. You will notice what fits with your values and what doesn't. Then you can deliberately build a life that is consistent with all that.

2 Live creatively.

We are creative beings. Our creativity is innate, built in by the fantastically creative universe. Don't limit yourself to a life of routine and predictability. Whenever possible, do something different; try something new. Seek out awe and inspiration. Find beauty everywhere. Be open to new possibilities. Try a different approach when it comes to dealing with relationship conflicts. Work in a unique way. Have fun, be silly; get playful. Through creative self-expression, we can learn a lot about ourselves. And when we know ourselves better, we live more authentically.

3 Learn to trust your gut feelings.

Our instincts – that so-called 'sixth sense'; – speak to us all the time. It's just that we rarely slow down long enough to notice. Pay attention to your gut feelings. Notice those instinctive reactions or thoughts that seem to come from nowhere.

Our inner voices often speak loudest when we are heading away from our true nature. We tend to feel uncomfortable, as if something isn't right. Perhaps we'll feel tension in our bodies. When you pay attention to these sensations, they can guide you back towards your authentic self – the one place that always feels comfortable.

4 Embrace your mistakes.

If you're unable to be accountable for your mistakes, or you spend time making excuses for your shortcomings or deny your weaknesses, you'll feel like a fake. We all have weaknesses, and even those who are really engaged in life will make a mess of things from time to time. Errors are part of the human experience and, when we acknowledge them, we can also see the wisdom they contain. This allows us to adapt and grow and step into our lives and ourselves more fully.

Remember this

Next time you catch yourself making a mistake, pause, take a deep breath and evaluate what happened. Then take time out for self-compassion. Acknowledge that good people make errors from time to time, treat yourself kindly and consider how you can avoid the mistake next time around. Then move on. Compassion allows us to try again. Self-directed criticism or anger keeps us too scared to try.

Key idea

Authenticity isn't something shaped by default. It takes deliberate attention, self-awareness and honest inquiry, but it can also be fun. When you begin living from this place of deep self-understanding, you're more likely to tap into your passion and purpose and feel more alive.

Discovering your passions

Once you are living a more authentic life, you are clearer about what matters to you, what drives you and all that inspires you. You are confident and ready to experience all that life has to offer. This vitality leads you straight into a life filled with passion and purpose.

Passion is enthusiasm for one, or sometimes several, pursuits. It is an excitement that compels you to take action, explore and engage in something purely because you love it or are inspired by it. When you are swept up in a passion, you feel alive and connected to the powerful energy of the universe. You may actually feel as though you've merged with higher consciousness, because you are drawing from source energy.

Defining purpose

Purpose evolves when we begin to know ourselves deeply and, in many ways, it helps us define who we are. It shows what we care about and what our contribution to the world will be. When we live close to our purpose, it feels natural and right – as though we're doing just what we're meant to do.

This is both a spiritual and a practical thing. The way to become clear about your purpose is to become clear about yourself. You will then discover the real-world actions you must take to express it.

THE DANCE BETWEEN PASSION AND PURPOSE

It's unlikely that you will ever discover a purpose that you aren't passionate about. The two are so interrelated that they grow and inspire each other. Passion often fuels purpose and purpose is what shapes our lives. When you know what your purpose is – when you are aware of your mission – you're likely to be passionate about the things you must do to fulfil it.

Your passions and purpose aren't always obvious. It takes patience, dedication and commitment to discover just what you are meant to do, but the process itself is enlightening.

Key idea

Passion is enthusiasm, adoration for something. Purpose is the unique expression of our ideas, talents and abilities in a way that fuels growth or understanding or contribution. It is what we are meant to do while on this planet.

The two qualities are interrelated. They flow out of and through each other. We are often passionate about our purpose, and we often discover our passions when we are aligned with what we are meant to do.

PURPOSE IS NOT ALWAYS THE EASY ROAD

You can get a glimpse of your purpose when you pay attention to what you like, what calls to you. However, don't be deluded into thinking the expression of purpose is always easy or always fun. It can be downright hard to do what we are meant to do, but it is always meaningful.

For example, Winston Churchill's purpose may have been to lead and inspire people to change a culture. There was nothing easy about that. Mahatma Gandhi's purpose was to lead others to peaceful self-empowerment. That purpose was expressed despite war, oppression and violence. That's a hard thing to do.

Still, it is not surprising that purpose, for many of us, often appears out of disparity or lack. When you become aware of the suffering and inequality in the world – as Mother Teresa and Nelson Mandela did before you – you may be compelled to ease that pain and poverty. In your efforts to ease suffering, you may stumble over the work you are meant to do.

When you find something that moves you, when you feel compelled and alive, you're on track toward purpose. Your purpose will require you to express your talents, skills and desires in a unique way, one that only you can provide. It is almost always bigger than you think it is and it usually becomes the thing that is impossible *not* to do.

PINPOINTING YOUR EXPRESSION OF PURPOSE

We long for a direction in life, a single, directed purpose. This is something that enables us to know what we're supposed to be doing, but our purpose is always more fluid and flexible than that. Even when you discover your purpose, there are numerous ways to express it and it's likely to shift and grow as you grow throughout your life.

To pinpoint your purpose, then, you must be open, aware and mindful. You also must be willing to work in co-operation with faith, because there will be times when you feel you are making no progress – that nothing is clear – and yet those fallow periods also hold the information you need to help make your purpose clear.

Try it now

Write down three things you love to do. Now explain your motivation for doing them. What is it that attracts you? Why do you like these things? What drives you? Write in your journal about this. Often it's the motivation behind what we do that leads us to purpose.

For example, you may like to cook nutritious meals. Perhaps you're motivated by the desire to create healthy foods for your family. Perhaps your purpose, then, centres on helping people live healthier lives.

Until you find what you are meant to do, keep exploring. Your purpose is probably lurking behind your passions and motivations.

THREE WAYS TO MOVE CLOSER TO PURPOSE

1 Mindfully explore life.

Try different things, be open to new experiences and play with your passions. Pay attention to the things that feel natural, intriguing and important. Notice how they mesh with your unique skills and look for ways to express those things.

2 Live actively and authentically.

Purpose does not evolve out of intellect. It evolves through trial and error, practice, study, experimentation and engagement. Discovering purpose is an active process. Throughout it, you'll discover much of what you don't want to do, what doesn't feel right, and what you aren't good at. This is all good information. Knowing what you don't want moves you closer to what you do.

Your purpose will be a true reflection of your authentic self. It will spin out of your skills and values and creativity. It's part of the energy of the universe. Your only job is to remain aware, open and engaged until you know deep inside that you are living on purpose.

Remember this

If you don't know what to do to identify your purpose, just do something. When we are immersed in life experience and exposed to different activities, ideas or challenges, we are often inspired to think creatively. That can foster the ideal conditions for purpose to take hold.

3 Look at the big picture.

Too often, we stumble across the things we love to do, the things we feel compelled to do and we think, 'Eureka, I've found my true purpose!' However, it's almost always bigger than what we discover. Our purpose is not limited or defined by our jobs or activities.

For example, you may love to teach and be passionate about your job, but that is not your purpose; it is only one expression of your purpose. Your purpose may, indeed, be to teach and encourage others, and school teaching is certainly one expression of that, but your purpose will also show in how you parent your children, relate to your spouse and coach the football team. There are numerous ways to teach and encourage others. There are always multiple ways to express your life's work.

If you love storytelling, entertaining and acting, your purpose may be to bring joy to others. You may express your purpose as a stage actor, a movie director or even a sales manager who uses all those skills to motivate employees.

Your purpose is never narrow or limiting. It is the full expression of who you are. When you are living an authentic life, connected to self, your passions and purpose will become illuminated. The expression of your purpose may shift and change as you awaken, but it will always require your unique set of skills and talents to express it.

It's your job to take on the task of discovering your passions and purpose and then connect to them in an authentic way. With this genuine expression of your authentic self, you will fulfil your purpose in a way that uplifts the entire world.

Focus points

* When we are living a life that is congruent with our true self – our values and priorities, our spiritual practices and actions – we are living an authentic life.
* Authentic people tend to be happier, have greater resilience, and a sense of meaning in their lives.
* Authenticity can also lead to an expression of purpose and passion.
* Purpose is what we feel we are meant to do while on this earth. It is an expression of our unique talents, abilities and desires.
* Purpose is always bigger than the roles or jobs that define it. It has various expressions and those expressions can shift and change as we change throughout our lives.

Next step

By living an authentic life you have tapped into your essence and discovered your passions and your purpose, an expression of your spirit. There is nothing mysterious about this process, nothing magical: it is simply a matter of paying attention and following your faith. In the final chapter, we'll explore some other ways of living a spiritual life towards self-actualization.

13

The varied path to enlightenment

In this chapter you will learn:

- ► *how to go boldly into spiritual practice*
- ► *six tips to enhance your daily practices.*

Going boldly into spiritual practice

The path to enlightenment, then, is about approaching each moment mindfully; it's about cultivating awareness and compassion and trusting that, when we do this, all we need to know will be illuminated. There is freedom in this because, when we detach ourselves from the outcomes, we become present to what is. We engage in life deeply, drop our resistance, and step into our faith and knowledge that things are just as they should be and that we are just where we must be.

Key idea

Living a spiritual life means accepting that everything is as it should be, and trusting that you'll receive the insight and wisdom you desire when you need it most. When you can live each moment from this place, you are awakening.

The spiritual practices in this book are written to help you reach this place of light and self-actualization, but they can also help you feel better – right now. While they offer intellectual understanding and a practical application for spiritual growth and exploration, these practices are inadequate on their own because enlightenment can be truly and honestly known only through experience.

BECOME PART OF THE LIGHT

Experience and illumination come from engagement and practice. Embrace these practices as you go forward. Engage in life. Build in healthy habits. Be a little bolder and braver than you were before. Be willing to confront your limiting beliefs and fears. Know that your life no longer has to be shaped by external influences and self-sabotage. Live authentically and quiet the noise of the unconscious.

When you are ready, release those old beliefs; surrender the ones that have become a source of pain and entrapment and step into the knowing that you are a part of the universal source. Then begin the next moment of your life from a state of curiosity and consciousness, compassion and love. This will ignite the spark of awakening. With practice, attention and awareness, that spark turns into a flame that ultimately lights up our entire life until we become part of the light aligned with all that is.

Key idea

Enlightenment can be known only through direct experience, but we can get glimpses of that light and live a healthier, happier life when we establish regular spiritual practices.

USE DAILY PRACTICE TO LIVE BETTER NOW

You can get there now. Enlightenment may occur in a moment or a lifetime but, by living a spiritual life, you can reap the benefits of good health and good feelings right now – on a daily basis. You can discover your purpose and make a positive difference in the world, and you can meet stress or hostility with love and compassion.

Commit to spiritual exploration and growth. Build in time for it and give attention to this dimension of life. It is the only one that really matters.

Six tips to enhance your daily practices

It matters less *what* you do and more that what you do you do mindfully and consistently. You must make a habit of compassion and awareness. You must get up and go outside to connect with all that is, in a direct way.

Whether you choose to embark on a practice of gratitude or meditation, whether you're going to pick up a book on mindfulness or whether you're learning about surrender, find what works for you and do it. Choose something that feels interesting and expansive and develop your own practice around it – one that is sustainable throughout your life.

Once you've started your practice, keep at it for at least 30 days before making a shift to something else. That's about how long it takes to shape a new habit that we can integrate into our daily lives.

Key idea

To live a spiritual life, you must develop habits that support spiritual growth. Regardless of which practices you choose, sustain them, explore them and commit to them to develop the habit in your life.

1 Exercise your body too.

Mind, body and spirit are all interrelated; therefore spirit is best expressed through a healthy body. Schedule time each day for physical exercise. Nourish your body with healthy food and activity. The healthier your body is, the sharper your mind will become and the more articulate your expression will be. Good health also creates the physical energy you need to express your purpose, live creatively, indulge your curiosity and serve others – all aspects of spiritual growth.

2 Find the awesome in your life.

On each step of your journey, take time to look for the awesome in your life and savour it. Search for the beauty and slow down long enough to appreciate it. See the goodness in others. Notice your awareness begin to expand and give thanks for that. Enjoy the love and compassion, not only that you receive, but also that you give. You can even find wisdom in troubling times – if you pay attention.

3 Appreciate the challenges.

Too often, we fight against our experience. We worry that things might not work out and we complain when things don't go our way. When something unexpected or undesirable comes to pass, ask for awareness. Learn what you can from the challenge and search for the gifts. This moves you out of victimhood and back into a place of possibility.

4 Connect each day with the divine.

Look for the divine in each day. It is there – because we are never separate from source. Seek out the signs of higher consciousness operating in your life. Get to know yourself as a spiritual being and feel the positive energy that emanates from that. Connect directly to the divine through prayer or meditation. Honour your intuitive hunches and enjoy the synchronicities. When you foster the connection, faith flourishes.

5 Study and seek support.

It's also helpful to study inspirational materials and discuss spiritual topics and questions with others. Find a group of like-minded people to talk over ideas, insights and questions. Form a book club, develop a study group, or create some other forum to discuss the spiritual topics that you are exploring.

The support of others can also help you through moments of confusion or doubt. And it's fun to be surrounded by a community of people who share your interests and can help you think about things in a new or different way.

6 Lead with love and compassion.

Finally, if you do no other thing, commit to living a compassionate life. Not only will you experience positive changes in your daily life, but you'll also help change the world for others. People are looking for relief on this planet and they are turning to spirituality – and the love and compassion it offers – to heal. Be a healing energy and draw on compassion to help yourself.

When you're feeling separate or suspicious, confused or hurt, misguided or disconnected, reach out to someone else. Help them. Sit with them through *their* pain. Be real and authentic and engaged in the experience and you'll discover that you feel better too. When we operate from the highest energies of the universe, we see that we are never separate from it.

Living with your essence

You don't have to change the way you are in order to live a spiritual life; you must simply commit to knowing yourself fully as an extension of spirit. Once you start living from that place, you will step into the light; you will know higher consciousness. You will be enlightened.

Taking it further

Further reading

Altman, D., *One-Minute Mindfulness: 50 Simple Ways to Find Peace, Clarity, and New Possibilities in a Stressed-Out World* (New World Library, 2011)

Belitz, C. and Lundstrom, M., *The Power of Flow: Practical Ways to Transform Your Life with Meaningful Coincidence* (Three Rivers Press, 1998)

Choquette, S., *The Power of Your Spirit: A Guide to Joyful Living* (Hay House, 2011)

Dyer, W., *Change Your Thoughts – Change Your Life: Living the Wisdom of the Tao* (Hay House, 2007)

Dyer, W., *Wishes Fulfilled: Mastering the Art of Manifesting* (Hay House, 2012)

Goddard, N., *The Power of Awareness* (DeVorss & Co., 2010)

Goddard, N., *Your Faith is Your Fortune* (DeVorss & Co., 2011)

Hanson, R., *Buddha's Brain: The Practical Neuroscience of Happiness, Love, and Wisdom* (New Harbinger Publications, 2009)

Hayes, S. and Smith, S., *Get Out of Your Mind and Into Your Life: The New Acceptance and Commitment Therapy* (New Harbinger Publications, 2005)

Hendricks, G., *Five Wishes: How Answering One Simple Question Can Make Your Dreams Come True* (New World Library, 2010)

Kabat-Zinn, J., *Full Catastrophe Living: Using the Wisdom of Your Body and Mind to Face Stress, Pain, and Illness* (Delta, 1990)

Kornfield, J., *Meditation for Beginners* (Sounds True Inc., 2008)

Langley, M., *Teach Yourself: Mindfulness Made Easy* (Hodder Education, 2011)

Lesowitz, N. and Sammons, M. B., *Living Life as a Thank You: The Transformative Power of Daily Gratitude* (Viva Editions, 2009)

Mitchell, S., *Tao Te Ching: A New English Version* (Harper Perennial Modern Classics, 2006)

Neff, K., *Self-Compassion: Stop Beating Yourself Up and Leave Insecurity Behind* (William Morrow, 2011)

Nepo, M., *The Book of Awakening: Having the Life You Want by Being Present to the Life You Have* (Conari Press, 2011)

Roszak, T., *The Voice of the Earth: An Exploration of Ecopsychology* (Phanes Press, 2011)

Sanchez, N. and Viera, T., *Take Me To Truth: Undoing the Ego* (John Hunt Publishing, 2007)

Schucman, H. (scribed), *A Course In Miracles* (Foundation for Inner Peace, 2008)

Seligman, M., *Flourish: A Visionary New Understanding of Happiness and Well-being* (Free Press, 2012)

Website addresses

The Internet is full of sites dedicated to spirituality, spiritual practices and personal development. Those listed below provide a broad and open perspective of spiritual practice and personal development ideas.

Beliefnet – inspiration, spirituality, faith: www.Beliefnet.com

Endless Satsung, a blog and site from spiritual teacher Nirmala: http://endless-satsang.com/nonduality-advaita-satsang-blog.htm

Imperfect Spirituality – extraordinary enlightenment for ordinary people; the author's site at www.imperfectspirituality.com

Psychology Today magazine: www.psychologytoday.com

DailyOM: Nurturing Mind Body & Spirit: www.dailyom.com

Spirituality & Health: http://www.spiritualityhealth.com/

Spirituality & Practice – Resources for Spiritual Journeys: http://www.spiritualityandpractice.com/

Index